A Diver's Guide To
Monterey
COUNTY, CALIFORNIA

BY BRUCE WATKINS

PUBLISHED BY **CALIFORNIA DIVING** news
SAINT BRENDAN CORP. HOME OF

Saint Brendan Corporation, P.O. Box 11231, Torrance, CA 90510
(310) 792-2333, FAX (310) 792-2336.

Printed in the USA by Rodgers & McDonald Graphics, Carson, CA

SPECIAL NOTE: The descriptions in this book are not scientific facts. The diver's final decisions and actions are their responsibility. The publishers and author of this book assume no responsibility of any mishap claimed to be a result of this book.

ISBN 0-9628600-1-8

Special Thanks to:

• Dan Burtis of Wet Pleasure Dive Shop,

• Captain Alan Cull of the *Pacific Star*,

• Captain Jon Cappella of Dive Boat *Xeno* and Tri Shark Charters,

• Dick Hunter of PacStar Charters,

• Captain Phil Sammet of the *Cypress Sea*,

• Captain Lyn May of the *Silver Prince*,

— to all of my friends who patiently modeled before my ever-present cameras, and to all of the divers who have shared their time, experience, and joy of the underwater world with me.

Dedication:
— To Carl Roessler of See & Sea Travel Service, who convinced me that I would hate diving with him if I did not bring along an underwater camera.

Contents

Sharpnose crabs.

California scorpionfish.

Forward

My mind drifts back to a peaceful dinner overlooking Monterey Bay. As the sun slowly set, the sky was ablaze with a hundred hues of red and orange. A flock of brown pelicans, silhouetted by the blazing sunset, glided along just above the surface of the glassy ocean. A raft of otters had just spun themselves up in a thick kelp bed for a evening's sleep, while the California sea lions were heading out to sea for a night of fishing. My buddy and I had just finished a fine seafood dinner and began to review the day's diving adventures. Images of octopuses, seals, and sunlight streaming through the kelp canopy flipped through my mind in a seemingly endless slide show. I was overwhelmed by how lucky I was to have such good diving, so close to home.

Yes, we are very lucky to have the opportunity to dive in Northern California. The grand experience of finning beneath a kelp canopy or the ability to dive with marine mammals and assorted large sharks can be memorable indeed. Sometimes, the little invertebrates that make diving here so colorful and interesting are often forgotten in the search for bigger thrills. However, the combination of big thrills, photogenic critters and an abundance of edible marine life makes Monterey County a true world-class dive destination.

Diver with bat stars.

Introduction

In this book I have attempted to describe all of the beach dive sites in Monterey County and many of the better sites that are accessible by boat only. Please do not feel slighted if I left out your favorite site or called it by a different name. I have named sites by the most common name known to me, although many sites go by several names. Often "boat only" sites are called by a different name by every captain who drops an anchor there. Also, it seems that the areas between well-known sites have been given separate names as well. I have deliberately provided more information for sites with easier access, because most of the divers who frequent these sites will benefit from the information. More advanced sites are covered in less detail because divers need to discover some things on their own.

Monterey County is a diverse piece of real estate that stretches from wide, sandy beaches in the north to the sheer cliffs of Big Sur in the south. In between are the historic Monterey Marina, the charm and ambiance of Cannery Row, the 17-Mile Drive, Carmel, and Point Lobos. This is a county of diversity and of the superlative. Words and photographs alone cannot capture the beauty and presence of Monterey. You must to go there and experience it yourself. Hopefully this book will be your guide to navigate through some of the best diving and spectacular scenery that California has to offer.

A Brief History of Monterey

Prior to 1600, the land that would become Monterey County was home to an assortment of Native Americans who went by the names of Ohlone, Esselen, and Salinan. These were peace-loving people who lived in small groups and foraged for fish and shellfish as well as deer, birds, and otters. Monterey was first "discovered" by Juan Rodriguez Cabrillo in 1542, although he never landed there. Sebastian Vizcaíno claimed the land for Spain in 1602, and named the area after his sponsor, the Conde de Monterey. During the Spanish period the Native Americans were rounded up into *rancherias*. Under confinement they rapidly became extinct through a combination of European diseases, for which they had no resistance, and interbreeding with the Spanish.

In 1834 much of the county was divided into Mexican land grants and the major ranches were established. Spanish rule came to an end in 1846 when U.S. Commodore John Drake Sloat annexed California to the United States. A constitutional convention was held in 1849 in Monterey to set up a Californian government, and statehood was established in 1850, with Monterey becoming the state's first capital.

Commercial fishing began during the 1850s, created mainly by Chinese immigrants, and developed into a thriving business. The Pacific Steamship Company built a wharf in 1870, later to be known as Fisherman's Wharf. Sardines, anchovies, squid, salmon, and abalone were harvested in record amounts. This colorful time in Monterey was captured in several books by John Steinbeck. Overfishing took its toll and several fisheries, particularly the sardines and basking sharks fisheries, collapsed during the 1950s.

Sport diving did not become popular until the 1960s, and the sport grew rapidly. Divers created a great awareness about the ocean and its inhabitants, and numerous game refuges and preserves were established. This activity peaked in 1993 with the establishment of the Monterey Bay National Marine Sanctuary.

The impact of marine life on tourism and particularly non-diving tourism is best exemplified by the Monterey Bay Aquarium. Hordes of visitors marvel at the diverse exhibits each year, and it has become the number one attraction in Monterey. The giant tanks have become a looking glass for non-divers to experience (at least partially) what we divers have known all along: the thrill of being underwater is without equal!

Some thoughts on Weather

While the The Mamas and the Papas might think that "It never rains in California," even the most overly optimistic Californians think of the weather here in terms of two seasons. There is a wet season when it is supposed to rain, but sometimes doesn't; and a dry season when it's not supposed to rain, but sometimes does anyway.

Divers, however, tend to think of California weather in three distinct diving seasons. During the spring and summer the Central Valley gradually heats up, drawing air and moisture off the ocean. These conditions produce steady, northwesterly winds, foggy beaches, and strong upwelling.

Much of Monterey county is near deep-water canyons of the continental shelf. Most notable of these is the Carmel Submarine Canyon that runs right up to shore at Monastery Beach. Upwelling occurs when winds drive surface water out to sea to be replaced by cold, nutrient-laden waters from deep within the canyons. This upwelling brings two essential factors together—sunlight and nutrients—

and the plankton thrives.

During spring and summer the surface temperatures can drop to a chilly 43-45° F, and the water turns the color and turbidity of green pea soup. Or, the water may turn a deep red due to the presence of specific types of dinoflagelets, a condition that is often called a "red tide." This upwelling and the resulting explosion of life is what makes makes Monterey marine life so diverse and rich.

During late summer through fall the northwesterly winds wane, and the water temperature climbs to its highest yearly values (high 50s to mid 60s during particularly warm years). This is the predictably best time to dive Monterey County. The visibility can generally be counted on to be quite good (30 to 60 feet), and the wind and wave action are very acceptable. Beaches are likely be be clear and sunny.

Winter can best be characterized as beauty and the beast. When the winter storms roll through California with their 70-mile-per-hour plus winds and 18-foot swells, it is best to view the ocean from a long, safe distance. However, the times between storms offer the absolutely finest conditions of the year. The sun is low in the sky, providing minimal light for water-clouding plankton. During these times the visibility may grow to 70 feet or more and occasionally over 100 feet. On these days Monterey County will put highly-rated tropical locations to shame.

On balance, the weather on the coast is highly changeable and somewhat unpredictable. Every now and then the little demons that mess with our weather do something really funky. At times their playfulness can result in spectacular disasters but other times can produce some mighty fine diving. For instance El Niño conditions (a warm, northward running current that occurs irregularly) often produce superior conditions with warm, clear water and an assortment of interesting critters brought up from Southern California.

Site Rating & Beach Diving Tips

I have adopted a system from my ski buddies to rate these dive sites. A beginner site (●) is one in which a newly certified diver, one who has not put a tank on for some time, or a diver who has little/no experience in California beach diving, is not likely to get into trouble. These sites have parking near the entry point and have predictably calm and less strenuous entries and exits.

Intermediate sites (■) are ones that should only be attempted if you have recent California beach diving experience and are in reasonably good

physical shape. Beginners should be comfortable here if they are with a more experienced diver.

Advanced sites (◆) should only be attempted by experienced California divers who are in good physical shape. There may be strenuous walks to the entry point or difficult beach/rock entries. Experience in reading ocean conditions is a must.

Difficult sites (◆◆) should only be attempted by the most knowledgeable/experienced California divers who are in excellent physical condition. These sites are characterized by difficult/strenuous entries and exits, often have long walks to the entry point, and have rough surface conditions and strong currents. Experienced divers should not bring novice divers along on these dives.

Note: Weather will influence the above rating system. A storm swell can turn the easiest entry into a double black diamond in less than an hour. Take some time to evaluate the conditions, and determine if you are comfortable with the conditions at a specific site on a specific day. It is always better to use your experience to choose not to dive, rather than rely on strength and skill to get you out of difficult situations.

These ratings are only applicable to beach entries. Those diving from their own boats should evaluate the conditions of the day against their own experiences. Passengers on charter boats should seek guidance from the captain.

First and foremost, diving is supposed to be fun! If you get in over your head and push your physical abilities, you are probably not having fun. Know yourself, your abilities, and your interests. Then decide if you will enjoy the dive at hand. It's perfectly all right to drive three hours to a site and blow off the dive due to non-optimal ocean conditions.

Typically, waves break on the beach in sets; that is, several small waves followed by a set of larger waves. Take 20 minutes or so to watch the ocean so you get an understanding of how the waves are breaking that day and how large the largest wave is likely to be. The self control to sit and watch, rather than immediately jump into your gear and go, may save you a good thrashing at the hands of an uncaring ocean.

Divers should enter during the periods of smaller waves. Enter the water with the regulator in your mouth, and turn and swim away from the beach. The trick is to traverse the surf line as quickly as possible. When exiting, again have the regulator in your mouth and crawl until you are well out of the surf line. This technique is known by locals as "The Monastery Crawl."

Dive Site Ratings

SITE NAME	BEACH DIVE RATING	VISIBILITY	FACILITIES	GAME	ACCESS	ENTRY
DEL MONTE BEACH	●	P	T, BL	VG	E	E
WHARF #2	■	P	T, BR	P	E	E
BREAKWATER	●	P	T, BR	P	E	E
HIDDEN BEACH	●	P	N	P	E	E
METRIDIUM FIELD	■	P	T	P	E	E, LS
MCABEE	●	P	N, BL	P	M	E
AQUARIUM REEF	Boat dive	F	N	P	B	B
HOPKINS REEF	Boat dive	F	N	R	B	B
LOVERS POINT	■	F	T, BL	L/F	M	M
OTTER COVE	■◆	F	N	L/F	M	M
CORAL STREET	■◆	G	N, BL	L/F	M	M
CHASE REEF	Boat dive	G	N	G	B	B
POINT PINOS	◆	G	N	L/G	M	VD
MOSS BEACH	◆	P	T	P	M	D
POINT JOE	◆	F	N	G	M	VD
CYPRESS POINT	◆	F	N	G	M	VD
LINGCOD REEF	Boat dive	G	N	G	B	B
PINNACLES	Boat dive	G	N	G	B	B
STILLWATER COVE	●	F	T	L/F	E	E
COPPER ROOF HOUSE	■◆	G	N, LP	L/G	M	D
BUTTERFLY HOUSE	■◆	G	N, LP	L/G	D	M
CARMEL RIVER BEACH	■◆	F	T, LP, BL	L/G	M	D
CARMEL MEADOWS	◆	G	N, LP	L/G	M	D
MONASTERY BEACH	◆	G	T, BL	L/F	E	D
MONO-LOBO	Boat dive	G	N	L/G	B	B
WHALERS COVE	●	G	T, BR	R	E	E
BLUEFISH COVE	■	VG	T, BR	R	E	E, LS
GIBSON BEACH	Boat dive	G	N	VG	B	B
WILDCAT CREEK	Boat dive	G	N	G	B	B
YANKEE POINT	Boat dive	VG	N	G	B	B
MALPASO CREEK	Boat dive	G	N	G	B	B
MILE MARKER 67	◆	G	N	G	D	D
WATERFALL BEACH	◆	G	N	G	D	D
MOBY LING COVE	◆	G	T	G	D	D
SOBERANES POINT	◆◆	VG	N	G	VD	VD
LOBOS ROCKS	Boat dive	VG	N	VG	B	B
REVERSE COVE	◆	G	T	G	VD	M
DIABLO PINNACLES	Boat dive	VG	N	G	B	B
VENTURA ROCKS	Boat dive	G	N	F	B	B
PARTINGTON COVE	◆◆	G	T	VG	VD	VD
SLATE ROCK	Boat dive	G	N	VG	B	B
LIMEKILN BEACH	■	F	T, C, BL	G	M	M
MILL CREEK	■	F	T, C, BL	VG	M	M
SAND DOLLAR BEACH	■	F	T	F	VD	M
JADE COVE	■◆	F	N	VG	VD	M
CAPE SAN MARTIN	Boat dive	G	N	VG	B	B

P	POOR	E	EASY
F	FAIR	M	MODERATE
G	GOOD	D	DIFFICULT
VG	VERY GOOD	VD	VERY DIFFICULT
		B	BOAT DIVE
T	TOILETS	LS	LONG SWIM
LP	LIMITED PARKING		
C	CAMPING		
BL	BOAT LAUNCH (for kayaks and small inflatables)	●	NOVICE
BR	BOAT RAMP (for larger boats)	■	INTERMEDIATE
N	NONE	◆	ADVANCED
		◆◆	EXPERT
R	RESERVE/NO HUNTING		
L	RESERVE/LIMITED HUNTING		

Boat dives difficulty varies according to conditions, see text for details

Many find rocky point entries a little scary the first time around, but become adept at it very quickly. Simply wait for the swell to come up to its maximum point, and one giant stride and two kicks later you are in deep water and far from the rocks. Take a little time to observe the area into which you intend to jump. The last thing you want to do is to skewer yourself on a rock that is lurking just below the surface.

Rocky beach exits are often easier in moderate waves than sandy beach exits. Simply swim up to the ledge with the regulator in your mouth and allow a wave to carry you up onto the rocks. Once on the rocks, either a short crawl or two steps will put you out of reach of the ocean. This is a lot easier than it sounds.

Beach divers are pushed back and forth by wave action and must expel a fair amount of effort getting past the surf line. On rocky entries the energy of the wave is directed up and down and tends to pick you up rather than smash you against the rocks. On particularly rough days you'll want to watch the wave pattern before approaching the rocks, and pick a time where the sets are at a low intensity. Alternatively, on calm days you'll want to ride the largest wave out of the water. A little experience in timing waves will allow you to get in and out with a surprising small amount of effort.

Remember, you are ultimately responsible for your safety, and your diving skills need to be weighed against the conditions *de jour*.

Summary of Monterey's Diving Regulations

Each year a great many well-meaning divers break the law and accrue heavy fines. Most of these divers do not intend to be criminals but are simply unaware of the changing and sometimes obscure laws that govern diving in Monterey County.

Some of these regulations are in response to the California Coastal Commission forcing the owners of privately-held property to allow access, and the owners' intent to allow as little access as possible. Others are intended to keep the best parking spots available to non-diving tourists. It would appear that the cities involved value non-divers more than divers and are actively discouraging divers from their cities.

What can divers do to to prevent further erosion of their access rights? First, obey the existing laws. Respect the rights of others on the beach, pick up your trash, and maybe somebody else's trash as well. Some may appreciate the view of your buns while crawling out of your wet suit, but many will not. Use the restrooms and changing rooms instead of the back seat of your car. Frequent the local shops and restaurants; let them know that you are a diver.

Right: Diver with blacksmith fish.
Below: Spanish shawl nudibranch.

Special Access Rules

City of Monterey. Parking lots throughout the Cannery Row area are marked with "changing and unloading permitted" or "prohibited" signs. Divers need to be careful to park in "legal" lots only and note that the lots located close to some of the better entry spots are the ones that are prohibited.

City of Pacific Grove, Lover's Point. From May 1 through September 30, on Friday through Monday, and Memorial Day, Independence Day, Labor Day and California Admissions Day, all diving activity on the east side of Lover's Point is prohibited. However, diving is permitted on the east side of the point southerly of the pier from sunset through 11:30 a.m. during the regulated time. All diving activities must be completed by 11:30 a.m. That means you and your gear must be off of the beach. Diving from November through April and on the west side of the point is unregulated. There is a fee for diving classes.

Stillwater Cove, Pebble Beach. Diving is limited to 10 divers per day; there are 6 parking spots that must be reserved up to 14 days in advance. There is a loading/unloading area, but incoming traffic is prohibited between the hours of 11 a.m. and 2 p.m. daily. There is a pier and boat hoist available for recreational craft only from May 1 through September 30, with a limit of 10 boats per day. Diving, sunbathing, and picnicking are permitted during daylight hours only, and only on the beach east of the pier. Spearguns are also prohibited. Call (831) 625-8536 for reservations and additional information.

Point Lobos State Reserve. Diving is limited to 15 teams of two divers per day. Reservations for diving are encouraged and may be obtained by leaving a voice mail message at the Reserve at (831) 624-8413 no sooner than two months in advance, or via electronic mail: ptlobos@mbay.net. You will then receive either an E-mail, FAX or postcard message that will direct you to send a check to the Reserve. If you did not make the first 15 teams, your message will be ignored. Divers are given a complete set of regulations when they register at the ranger station. The park opens at 9 a.m.

Partington Cove. Diving in Partington Cove is by permit only; call (831) 667-2315 for information. Divers need to submit an application listing the names and certification of all divers, pay a fee, and name the State of California payable on an insurance policy.

Jade Cove. There are no diving regulations here, but there is a prohibition against taking jade. California state law strictly prohibits the taking of jade above the high tide mark, and the state requires a permit to remove minerals (e.g., mine) from the sea floor. The regulations of the Monterey Bay National Marine Sanctuary prohibit the state from issuing such permits. The removal of jade is therefore illegal, although there is a move afoot to change the law and make recreational jade collection legal.

Artifact Hunting. The state of California claims ownership of all wrecks in offshore waters. It is illegal to remove artifacts from wrecks, particularly historic wrecks, without a permit. Contact the state for more information: California State Lands Commission, Submerged Cultural Resources Unit, 1807 13th Street, Sacramento, CA 95814.

Marine Conservation Laws

In addition to the California Department of Fish and Game Laws that apply state-wide, the Monterey area has established a set of even stricter regulations. Many of these are intended to preserve the underwater environment for all to experience, minimize the impact of divers, and prevent overfishing.

Monterey Bay National Marine Sanctuary. This National Marine Sanctuary was dedicated in 1993 and encompasses all of the waters described in this book. Contrary to the name, the sanctuary does not regulate either sport or commercial fishing. It does prohibit mining the sea floor and drilling for oil, prohibits certain kinds of ocean dumping, and makes stronger other existing laws to protect marine mammals, birds, and turtles. It also prohibits thrill craft (jet skis) in all but a few designated areas.

For divers the biggest impact has been to those who liked to dive for jade (see above) and for photographers trying to get up close and personal with their subject. The Sanctuary has amended its rules to prohibit the attraction of great white sharks by any method within three miles of shore and within the Monterey Bay itself (Sanctuary waters only). The prohibition is in the same waters where it is illegal to angle for and kill white sharks by state law.

Divers are warned not to approach any marine mammal closer than 50 feet and not to cause them to deviate from their normal behavior.

Hopkins Marine Life Refuge. Intended to protect the subtidal and intertidal research programs, the Hopkins reef system has been designated a Marine Life Refuge. The protected area extends from the mean high tide mark out to a depth of 60 feet and is bordered by the Pacific Grove/Monterey Boundary (near the Monterey Bay Aquarium) on one side and by Third Street in Pacific Grove on the other. No marine life may be taken within the reserve, except by special permit issued by the Hopkins Marine Station. Diving is currently permitted in the reserve for divers entering the reserve by boat. Access to the reserve from the beach is prohibited as is landing a vessel or walking along the shore unless you have permission from the Refuge Manager. Researchers at the Hopkins Marine Station request that boats not anchor in the reserve and divers not disturb experiments on the sea floor. The Marine Station is considering new rules to require divers to register prior to entering the reserve, so watch for changing regulations. If hunting in deeper water be careful not to take game shallower than 60 feet. Contact the reserve Manager for more information: Hopkins Marine Station, Pacific Grove, CA 93950; phone, (831) 655-6200.

Pacific Grove Marine Gardens Fish Refuge. From Third Street in Pacific Grove to the Pacific Grove City limits near Asilimar Conference Grounds, from the high tide mark out to a depth of 60 feet, no invertebrate or plant life may be taken. It is legal to take fin fish.

Carmel Bay Ecological Reserve. East of a line drawn between Pescadero Point on the 17-Mile Drive to Granite Point in Point Lobos State Reserve, no invertebrates may be taken. It is legal to take fin fish.

Point Lobos State Reserve. Within the limits of the reserve, nothing, and I mean nothing, may be taken or disturbed. The northern boundary of the underwater area is a line drawn north, northwest from the western side of Granite Point. The southern Reserve boundary is the line drawn due west from the stone house directly south of the mouth of Gibson Creek. Divers should obtain an accurate description of the reserve boundaries from one of the Point Lobos Rangers at (831) 624-4909

Game Diving

Catching one's dinner is a popular diving activity throughout Monterey county. While the popular sites along Cannery Row and Carmel Bay are fished out, there is still plenty of game to be found at less popular sites and at sites that can only be reached by boat. Divers should recognize that the ocean's bounties are not endless, and they should take only what they need. In a time of dwindling resources, killing for killing's sake is no longer acceptable. Divers should be aware of Department of Fish and Game Laws, and follow them. Beyond these laws there is a code of honor among divers that should be followed. Take only what you intend to eat, and eat what you take. Never shoot a fish unless you are sure it is good to eat, and always choose the right equipment so that you will kill, and not just wound, your quarry. A California sport fishing license is required to take game and may be ordered by calling (916) 227-2244. Shellfish health advisories are available from the Department of Health Services at (510) 540-2605.

> **California Fish and Game Regulations are subject to change and, especially in recent years, have changed considerably from year to year, even month to month. Consult the latest fish and game regulations pamphlet or visit the regulations web page at www.dfg.ca.gov/title/d1_c4_a1.html.**

Diver with rose anemone.

Introduction to Monterey Bay

More tanks are emptied along the eastern side of Monterey Peninsula than any other location in Northern/Central California. The peninsula effectively protects these entry points from the prevailing northwesterly wind and swell, and the area has an abundance of interesting critters to dive with. Sites include the vast

A diver explores under a thick kelp canopy.

expanse of Del Monte Beach, where instructors find calm water for their students and where hunters find trophy halibut, several notable sites along Cannery Row, and the rugged, rocky beaches of Point Pinos.

Much of the ambiance of present day Monterey derives from the lowly sardine. Beginning in the early 1900s Monterey became known for its world-famous fishing and canning industry. The industry peaked in 1945 and crashed in 1951 due to overfishing, but not before Monterey Bay gave up millions of tons of the little fish.

The heyday of the canneries gave us the Pulitzer Prize-winning John Steinbeck and his classic novels *Tortilla Flat*, *Sweet Thursday*, and, of course, *Cannery Row*. Things have changed a bit since the 1940s. The canneries are no longer working, and many of the old buildings have been replaced by modern hotels. Visitors will find that the ambience of old Monterey is alive in the historic buildings of Fisherman's Wharf and Cannery Row. This area has an abundance of attractions: fine restaurants; wildlife viewing; the Monterey Bay Aquarium; the Allen Knight Maritime Museum; and, of course, numerous dive sites.

In this short stretch of coastline I include ten beach entry points as well as five "boat-only" sites. Of course there are more, but I've limited myself to the more common sites with name recognition. Most of the beginner sites in Monterey County are included in this protected area and most of these sites are accessible from shore, without the need of a boat. Those who own their one small boat or kayak will have access to every site discussed within. Two marine life refuges currently exist in Pacific Grove: the Hopkins Marine Life Refuge and the Pacific Grove Marine Gardens Fish Refuge. There is pending legislation to create the Edward F. Ricketts Ecological Reserve along Cannery Row.

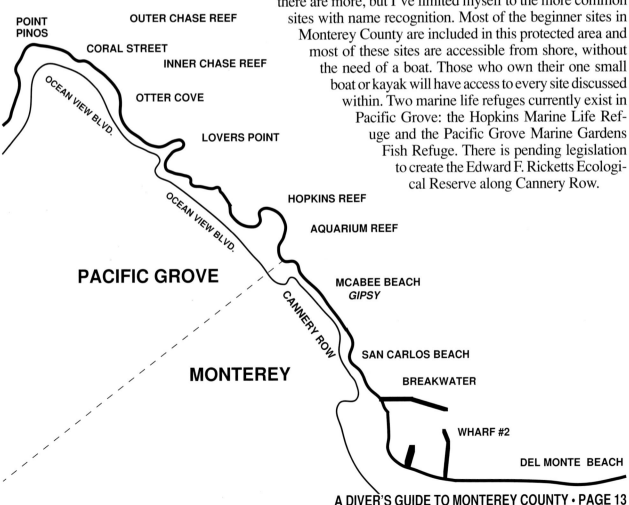

POINT PINOS

OUTER CHASE REEF

CORAL STREET

INNER CHASE REEF

OCEAN VIEW BLVD.

OTTER COVE

LOVERS POINT

OCEAN VIEW BLVD.

HOPKINS REEF

AQUARIUM REEF

PACIFIC GROVE

CANNERY ROW

MCABEE BEACH
GIPSY

SAN CARLOS BEACH

MONTEREY

BREAKWATER

WHARF #2

DEL MONTE BEACH

Del Monte Beach

There is a wide, sandy beach that stretches along Monterey Bay from the county line, near Moss Landing, right up to Wharf #2. This beach goes by many names: Moss Landing State Beach, Marina State Beach, Monterey State Beach. But divers collectively refer to the southern stretch of this beach as Del Monte. The beach is bordered by ice plant-covered dunes and groves of tall eucalyptus trees and is a great place to beach comb, picnic, or just catch a few rays. Offshore, divers find a habitat that is unique to the Monterey Area.

The waters near the wharf are almost always calm due to the protection of the wharf and breakwater. It is, therefore, no surprise that this part of Del Monte Beach is a favorite location to take students on their first dive. The calm conditions and flat bottom also makes this a perfect location for advanced students to practice navigation skills.

In the shallow water (10-15 feet) near shore lie extensive beds of sand dollars. As the water deepens a bit, the sand gives way to fields of eel grass. Within the protective environment of the eel grass are numerous juvenile fish and an assortment of tiny nudibranchs that are unique to this habitat.

Beginning about 200 yards offshore from Wharf #2 and running parallel to shore to near the Monterey Beach Hotel is a large shale reef. This patch of ocean is sometimes referred to as Tanker Reef or Shale Beds. The sea floor here consists of a series of shale ledges running parallel to shore. Attached to this meager rocky foundation is a thin forest of kelp consisting of both bull and giant kelp.

Within the tiny crevices of the shoals are found a few octopus and a few small fish.

The shale is at-tacked by a species of clam that rasps away burrows into the soft shale by holding onto the shale with its foot and using its shell as a scraping tool. Beachcombers often find pieces of shale on the beach decorated with neatly drilled holes. This natural art is a result of many years of boring clam activity.

Directly off Del Monte Beach near the Monterey Bay Kayak entry point is the shell of a Buffalo half track. The crumbling remains of this armored personnel carrier make for an interesting search and navigation activity for advanced classes and for photographers. The wreck has acquired a growth of anemones, scallops, and other invertebrates. It lies in 20 feet of water in an eel grass bed about 1/4 mile offshore. The wreck may be located by lining up the "Y" in the light-colored tree to the east of the entry point with the "T" in the Tynan Lumber Company sign. At the same time line up the chimney on the first building on Wharf #1 with the dome-shaped statue up on the hill above Monterey. There is also a wreck of a sailboat nearby, but the lightweight boat moves around a lot.

Del Monte Beach stands out as the best location in Monterey County for hunting halibut. The entire Del Monte beach area is good for hunting halibut, and the fish tend to move around in loosely associated groups. Some divers prefer to scuba dive in 20-40 feet of water, while others like to free dive just off the surf line. The submerged remains of a wrecked pier lie about 200 yards west of the intersection of Park Street with Del Monte Beach, and halibut tend to be herded into shallow water by this structure.

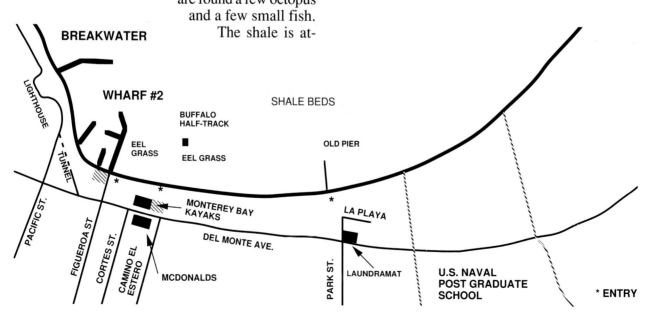

Access, Entry and Hazards: There are many access points to Del Monte Beach. Divers may park in the metered lot at the foot of Wharf #2 and enter near the wharf. Alternatively, there is a fee lot to the right of the Monterey Bay Kayak store at the intersection of Del Monte Avenue and Camino el Estero. This part of the beach is sometimes called "McMuffin" due to the proximity of McDonald's Restaurant. Divers may also try entering near the intersection of La Playa and Park Avenue, an entry known by old timers as "The Laundromat." There is limited, free parking available. Divers with small boats prefer to hunt in the waters off the new California State University, Monterey Bay (formerly Fort Ord). This area receives less diver traffic than other sites along Del Monte Beach since there is no shore access. Divers should watch for boat traffic.

Hunting the Northern California Halibut

So you're looking for a little excitement. Maybe searching for slow-moving abalone is losing its thrill; or you're bored with shooting 12-inch surf perch. If you're looking for a real challenge, try something really big. Try bagging a halibut.

While scientists use the Latin name *Paralichthys californicus*, divers refer to these enormous fish as "hallies" or "flaties." No matter what you call them, the California halibut is one of the most sought-after game fish by California spearfishers, and with good reason. It is the largest of the commonly speared fish and can grow up to be 5 feet long and weigh over 70 pounds. Fish in the 40-to 50-pound range are regularly taken by spearfishers. They are also one of the most challenging fish to locate and bag. Their camouflaged pattern blends in very well with their sandy-bottom habitat and many divers, both novice and expert alike, swim over many fish without ever noticing. Once a large fish is speared, the real challenge is subduing the fish and getting it back to the beach or boat.

A diver subdues a large halibut.

California halibut range along the Western United States from Washington State to Baja, and are found on mud and sand bottoms from the surf line to well over 600 feet. They may be identified by their rather large mouth; both eyes are usually, but not always, on the left side of the head; and the maxillary (upper jaw) extends past the eye. During the fall and winter halibut feed in deep water on squid, anchovies, and queenfish. Beginning about February the fish move inshore to depths of 60 feet or less for spawning, which lasts through July.

Newly hatched halibut are pelagic and drift at the mercy of the currents. At this stage the young fish appear much like other fish; that is, they have an eye on each side of their head. During the next 20 to 30 days the fish begin to change. The right eye slowly migrates to the left side of the head; and the right, eye-less side becomes pale as the eyed-side takes on the halibut's characteristic camouflaged pattern. Occasionally nature makes a mistake and the left eye is the one that migrates, or either a camouflaged pattern or the pale coloration develops on both sides. When the fish reach about 10 mm in length, they abandon their pelagic life and migrate into shallow bays and estuaries.

After the spawning season the adult fish remain in shallow water and June through September is the most productive time for spearfishers to seek these fish while they are found at depths to 60 feet. They are often found just beyond the surf line. In Northern California the height of the halibut season is June through August.

Divers should swim as far off the bottom as the visibility permits and look for the pattern of the fish on the sand bottom. Initially, the challenging part is recognizing the fish as you swim over it. Often the fish will bury itself under a thin layer of sand with only their eyes exposed, while at other times they will be found lying in plain view. Their camouflaged coloration makes them difficult to distinguish from the sand bottom. Learn to be able to pick the "halibut-shaped" pattern out of the patterns of ripples in the sand. Where one fish is found there are usually more nearby.

Remember that leaving a wounded fish to slowly die will get no one a medal of honor. Only shoot fish that you have both the equipment and skill to land. Attempting to land a 50-pounder with a pole spear will only get the spear broken, yourself injured, and will probably end up feeding a group of sea stars when the wounded animal finally dies. A number of dive shops in the Monterey and San Francisco Bay areas offer speciality classes on spearfishing. If you've never gone after these big fish before, it may be best to take one of these classes or to find a veteran hunter to dive with.

Wharf #2

I navigated among a maze of pillars that supported a ceiling some 30 feet above. Blackness engulfed me except for a distant green glow silhouetting so many Grecian columns. The noon sun challenged the darkness but was overwhelmed in a soup of microscopic algae. When I turned on my dive light, the pillars exploded in a kaleidoscope of color. Each column was draped in a royal tapestry of living creatures—reds, greens, lavender and pure white. The color was simply breathtaking.

Wharf #2 in Monterey Harbor is a location often visited by divers, but rarely dived. This is the very same spot where divers line up each morning to be swept off to distant dive sites by Monterey's fleet of charter dive boats. Few, however, take the time to consider what kind of diving could be directly beneath their feet as they sip coffee and wait for their

White anemones cover many of the pilings under the pier.

boat. In fact, the owner of a popular charter boat claims that Wharf #2 is the very best dive in Monterey Bay.

The structure and pilings of the wharf provide a substrate for a host of invertebrate life to cling to and flourish. Each of the pilings seems to have its own personality and assortment of life. Some are covered from the waterline to the bottom with a lush carpet of Corynactis anemones. Individual colonies may be fluorescent red, bright orange, lavender, or even shades of pink. Other pilings are covered with snow-white anemones of the genus *Metridium*. Other columns are covered on their upper portions with the aggregating anemones, *Anthlopleura elegantissima*, their short stalks being well adapted to a rough and turbulent life in the intertidal range.

The wharf does have its share of larger creatures as well. Hanging upside down on the upper portions of the pilings may be found an occasional sheep crab. These large crabs may be some two feet across and appear like some giant underwater vulture waiting to pounce.

The calm waters provide a nursery for many of the larger fish. I have never seen so many lingcod in one place, none over about 14 inches long and many under 10 inches. Noting that this is far below legal minimum size, this is not a hunter's paradise, but it is a pretty good spot for fish portraits. Other fish such as cabezon, various species of flatfish, and rays may be found here in miniature versions. All in less than 25 feet of water.

With all of the interesting marine life and calm conditions the wharf is a macro photographer's dream. On the pilings may be found a host of little critters that feed on, and find shelter among, the many species of anemones. The smaller species of Metridium anemone seems to have a particular attraction for the local red octopus. Scan the Metridium covering, or gently run your fingertip between the anemones. Chances are in a very short time you will have disturbed a sleeping octopus. I firmly believe that any dive with an octopus is a good dive. They gracefully dance, change colors, and slip through your fingers. It is nothing short of joyous when they choose to extend a tentacle and investigate a bubble-blowing intruder.

The wharf is home to some of California's noisiest marine mammals—the California sea lions. Most of the time they may be found sleeping well above the water on the support structure of the wharf. This puts them well out of sight of tourists and can only be seen by passing boaters and divers. Normally they'll just keep one eye on an approaching diver and fade off to sleep after he/she has passed by. Other times they'll join divers in the water and perform a mini seal-ballet for their most appreciative audience. There is a concrete platform underneath the dock where the charter dive boats load up. At low tide there is often a single or small group of juvenile sea lions sleeping there. The youngsters will often put their noses right on your face mask and peer inside. Many of these sea lions have never seen divers up close and are as curious about the divers as the divers are of them.

Interesting thing about wharves: people drop things off them. This one is no exception and the bottom is littered with remains of past human activity: soft drink bottles, transistor radios, old shoes, shopping carts, fisherman's knives. Treasure hunters will find delight in poking around in the layers of history. Some even find old bottles or valuable pieces of jewelry. Be patient, have a keen eye, and you'll never know what you'll find.

Access, Entry and Hazards: Most divers gain access to the wharf by entering the water on the east side of the wharf, the far west end of Del Monte Beach. This is the calmest entry in the world, and divers need only surface swim out to the spot where the concrete abutment ends before submerging. Once under the wharf navigating is quite easy as the pier is much longer than it is wide, and it is always possible to see daylight on either side. Divers may also anchor their boat off the west side of the wharf and gain access by a short, **underwater** swim.

A word of caution: this is not a dive for beginners. While the water is shallow, 30 feet maximum, and the conditions are the calmest in the bay, there are many hidden hazards. The wharf is frequented by sport fishers and monofilament fishing line is everywhere, along with a discarded gill net. Carry a sharp knife! The wharf has many sharp protrusions to cut an unsuspecting diver, and small boats take shortcuts by passing beneath the wharf. This is not the place for an unobservant diver. Also, it is wise to keep your distance from the many that are fishing with hook and line. They get upset when they see bubbles around their fishing line.

Divers must obtain permission form the harbor master before diving underneath Wharf #2, and it is not permitted to dive within the marina itself. The harbor master is concerned for your safety and will check to see if any construction activities are planned that day. The harbor master is under no obligation to grant permission, so ask politely.

The Breakwater

Many of us remember the breakwater as the location of their first ocean scuba dive. Indeed, this dive site is one of the most protected from ocean swells in the Monterey Bay area and is an ideal spot for open-water check-out dives. Most divers, however, migrate away from the breakwater as their diving skills improve, to find more challenging sites, to avoid the crowds, and to search for game. As more and more divers take up underwater photography the breakwater has become renowned for its incredible collection of photogenic marine life. Even within an area that is well known for its excellent macro photography, the breakwater stands out as one of the best!

This dive site is most easily recognized by the large breakwater/wharf which extends out from the parking lot. The Coast Guard operations building is at the near end of the parking lot, and their boats are kept alongside the main wharf. On the south

Corynactis or strawberry anemones.

side of the wharf is a large marina with boat-rental facilities, a boat-launching ramp, a deli, and dive shop.

Divers enter the water from San Carlos Beach on the north (ocean side) of the breakwater. From the beach extends a sand bottom which gradually slopes down to a maximum depth of 60 feet along the 400 yards of the breakwater. While generally uninteresting, the sand bottom is dotted with sand dollars, sea pens, and *Anthopleura* anemones, many of which have intricately colored radial disks. Translucent tentacles of white, orange and purple burrowing anemones wave to and fro in the surge.

To the left of the breakwater stretches a rocky patch reef that extends all the way to McAbee Beach. Here divers will find kelp-covered rocks with an interesting assortment of hermit crabs, small fish, and nudibranchs.

The breakwater itself was fabricated from large granite blocks, and these blocks create a labyrinth of small crevices and passageways in which a virtual army of sea creatures can find a home. The best diving is along the rock pile which

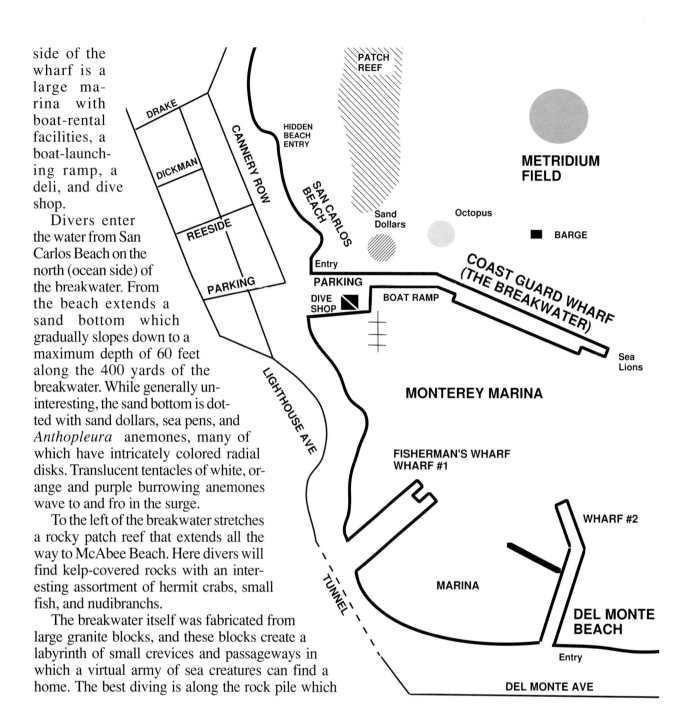

The breakwater is very popular and can get crowded with divers.

makes up the structure of the breakwater itself. The visibility is not as good here as other, less protected areas in Monterey, but the abundance of marine life more than makes up for the lower visibility.

Striped shrimp hang on the underside of rocky ledges and monkeyface-eels peer out of holes. In many areas the rocks are covered with a lush carpet of strawberry anemones that make interesting subjects for macro photographers. These little anemones possess fluorescent pigments in their tissues and cause rocks to appear as if they were glowing.

Numerous fish-eating anemones with their bright red bases, as well as the giant green anemone, are common near the end of the breakwater. Small shrimp, juvenile abalone, and an assortment of small crabs will make macro photographers think that they are in heaven. Living on, and feeding on, the kelp itself are an assortment of photogenic subjects, including the brilliantly colored purple-ring top snail and bright red kelp crab.

One of the biggest attractions that the breakwater has to offer is the large colony of California sea lions that congregate there. The last half of the breakwater itself is not accessible to people from the wharf and is a favorite hauling-out location of these large and noisy mammals.

Diving with marine mammals can certainly be a delightful experience, but one should not pass up seeing the small delicate creatures as well. One of the most beautiful groups of marine creatures are the nudibranchs and a great many species can be found in this area.

Access, Entry, and Hazards: Divers can park in the lot at the foot of the breakwater, on the street, or in the large lot up the hill. Bring plenty of quarters for the meters or ticket machines. Walk down the stone stairs and enter between the breakwater and the rocks to the left. Alternatively, divers may gain access to the far end of the reef via the small park between the Monterey Bay Inn and Monterey Plaza Hotel. This little beach has a protected entry and is sometimes called "Hidden Beach." The Aquarius Dive Shop is in the breakwater parking Lot, and the Monterey Bay Dive Center is across the street from the Hidden Beach entry.

Night Diving

While the breakwater is a wonderful palace to dive during the day, the area has a rebirth at night. I define a good night diving location as one where you can observe creatures that are not normally seen during the day. And this one has a lot. The labyrinth created by the piled rocks is an oversized condominium for the creatures of the night. Crabs, shrimp, brittle stars, monkeyface-eels, and octopuses all emerge from the rocks as the sun sets.

As night dives go this one is a particularly easy one to plan. The city lights as well as the street lights on the wharf provide ample light for gearing up and for topside navigation, while underwater the wharf itself provides a constant point of reference. The best area to look for many of the night creatures is on the second half of the breakwater on the ocean side, while the best area to play with octopuses is in the sandy areas near the bend in the wharf. Look for octopus in the open, or mostly buried in the sand with only their eyes protruding.

Those who have never attempted night diving may want to give it a try. The colors at night appear much more brilliant than during the day. This is because the water selectively removes color from sunlight, while the light from your flashlight travels a shorter distance through the water and is less effectively filtered.

Metridium Field

Most Monterey divers search for kelp beds to find good diving. While the presence of kelp is a good sign that there is a healthy, rocky reef to be found underneath, the absence of kelp does not necessarily mean that there is only a boring, sand bottom to be found.

Throughout the Monterey Bay are patches of shale and rock that do not support any kelp at all; rather, they are covered with fields of white-plumed anemones, better known by their Latin name, *Metridium*. There are several of these "Metridium fields" in the Monterey Bay, but the most well known is located just north of the breakwater.

Here, surrounded by a sand bottom, is a large rock outcropping covered with hundreds of white-plumed anemones *(Metridium giganteum)*. They appear as large, pure white cotton balls which stretch out to the limit of visibility. On a clear day the white anemones appear to go on forever, although they only cover perhaps 50 yards square. This is an awesome spot for wide-angle photography when the water is clear.

The Metridium field is home to a great many animals. Octopuses hide among the anemone stalks, and

Top: Metridium anemones. Middle: Rose anemone. Bottom: Hilton's nudibranch.

large lingcod and cabezon try to hide under the anemones' tentacles. Numerous nudibranchs and shrimp also may be found at the bases of the anemones.

A bit inshore of the Metridium field and closer to the breakwater is the wreck of an old barge. The wreck sits in 65 feet of water, and may be located by lining up the radio tower on McAbee Beach with the third smoke stack inshore from Aquarium Reef. Then line up the light pole at the end of the roadway on the breakwater with the large, cream-colored hotel in downtown Monterey. The rail of the barge rises about five feet off the bottom, and the deck is partially intact. The vessel is covered with Metridium and other anemones and is a good spot for macro photography. Within the barge live a family of wolf eels. They may be coaxed from their home with frozen squid.

Access, Entry, and Hazards: Divers may enter at the foot of the breakwater and swim several hundred yards to the dive spot. It is located at the intersection of a line drawn to extend nearby Reeside Street and a line connecting Point Cabrillo and the tip of the breakwater. This is a long swim to the site and most divers use a boat to get there. Divers should watch for boat traffic. Divers should also carry a float with dive flag should they choose to swim out from shore.

McAbee Beach

Cannery Row offers interesting dive sites with extremely easy access. Most notable of these is McAbee Beach. This wide, sandy beach is located just behind Cannery Row between Hoffman and Prescott Avenues. It is almost always calm at McAbee since the Monterey Peninsula and Point Pinos protect McAbee Beach from the prevailing northwest swell. Consequently, you will see a number of dive classes here, particularly on weekends.

Divers follow the path from the sidewalk next to the El Torito Restaurant and proceed to the middle of the sandy beach. Entries are a breeze in the small-to-no surf, and a short swim will put you in 20 feet of water. The bottom near shore consists mostly of sand, giving way to rock and sand. As one proceeds deeper, a rock and boulder bottom predominates.

The calm waters offer a home to a number of the ocean's critters. Lemon nudibranchs and ringed dorids can be seen slowly looking for a quick dinner. One of the more interesting dorid nudibranchs is quite common here—the Hopkins Rosc. This hot pink nudibranch rarely grows to over one inch and makes for good photography if you own a camera that will photograph down to a 1:1 reproduction ratio.

The rocks are covered with an assortment of brightly colored invertebrates: sponges, anemones,

Squid Diving

For much of the year the market squid *(Logo opalescens)* ride the currents of the high seas, constantly searching for food. In the early summer the urge to reproduce grows stronger than the urge to feed, and squid by the millions migrate to Monterey Bay. Their sole purpose is to mate and lay eggs.

The opposite sexes perform an elegant ballet during the mating and courtship ritual, and afterwards the female produces translucent finger-like egg sacks—some four to six inches long. These are carefully attached to burred rocks on the sand bottom. As more squid lay their eggs, the cases produce enormous "flowers" that can be three or four feet across and contain hundreds of egg sacks, each containing two-hundred or so individual eggs. The squid die quickly after mating and the dying and mating squid become the main course for a feeding orgy. Sea lions, blue sharks, bat rays, and torpedo rays all join in on the feast.

Divers along Cannery Row in Monterey often see these mounds of squid eggs in shallow water but rarely see a single squid. That is, of course, because squid only come up to diveable depths at night and most divers don't frequent the spots of optimum squid concentrations at night. To see squid you must go to where they are when they are there, and have the right equipment.

A bright light is required and should be hung just above the bottom. Divers need to wait for a half hour or so until the squid congregate. Normally there are tons of squid eggs on the sand bottom. Sometimes there are few squid, but those few exhibit typical squid behaviors. They are often wonderful hams. Some jet along the bottom and pose patiently. Others may be intertwined in the mating act and are completely oblivious to cameras. Female squid are often seen carrying their precious egg cases around in search of the perfect place to attach them. That perfect place may be in front of your camera. Perhaps they are drawn to the light, or perhaps they enjoyed the extra vision provided by dive lights. Either way all you have to do is lay on the bottom and wait for the squid to seek you out.

At other times the squid experience can be overwhelming. Divers may find themselves in schools so thick that it is difficult to see your buddy only a few feet away. Imagine yourself in a swirling mass of squid, all jetting by with nervous impatience in their search for a mate!

Access, Entry, and Hazards: Boat Dive Only. Best squidding occurs in water around 85 to 90 feet deep off Monterey's Cannery Row. The squid runs occur each summer sometime between June and September. Watch for boat traffic. This is a deep dive, so divers should pay attention to decompression limits. For commercial squid charters call: (831) 372-3200.

Market squid.

and tunicates. A number of small (read undersized) abalone may be found deep in cracks and under ledges. This is sea otter country and those abalone who wander out side of their crack are quickly consumed.

There is no abalone hunting here for divers. In fact, there is little game here at all. Sport and commercial fishing pressure over the years has taken its toll. I occasionally see a worthwhile fish taken here. However, mostly I see inexperienced spearfisher taking small (and sometimes legally undersized) fish. Some fish are meant to be looked at and photographed and not killed. If you want to hunt game you would be better off at another location.

For those who are interested in sightseeing or photography McAbee can be a lot of fun. Sea otters are common here and will often swim up and check out a diver. On one night dive I watched an otter come up to a diver, put a paw on each side of the diver's mask, and peer in. An encounter such as that can make your whole week.

You'll find a number of lengths of eight-inch pipe strewn along the bottom. These are not from a shipwreck, but rather from the days of the sardine canneries. The old fishing boats would tie off to an off-

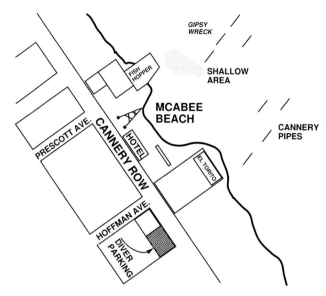

shore mooring, and the pipes were used to pump the sardines from the boat to the factory.

Access, Entry and Hazards: You should park in the lot diagonally across the street from the El Torito Restaurant and walk the short distance to the beach. The north end of the beach is bordered by a series of shops and restaurants, notably the Fishhopper Restaurant. Watch for boat traffic and fishing line.

Wreck of the SS Gipsy

McAbee Beach is also known as the resting place of the *SS Gipsy*. The *Gipsy* was a 239-ton, wooden-hull steamship. Under the command of Captain Leland she made the run between Monterey and San Francisco for nearly 30 years. She was so reliable that the nickname "Old Perpetual Motion" was aptly applied, and her captain was said to have known every rock and reef along the coast.

On September 27, 1905, Captain Leland took a much-deserved vacation and put the vessel in the hands of Captain Boyd, a good sailor, but inexperienced with Monterey. He mistook the buoy off China Point, where Hopkins Marine Station is today, for the entrance to Monterey Harbor. The ship ran aground and died a slow death in the rocks and surf. However, the soldiers from the Presidio were said to have thoroughly enjoyed the 400 cases of bottled beer and 100 kegs of steam beer that washed ashore.

There is little to see of the wreck today as some salvage was done and the wooden parts didn't last long. The boiler can still be found off the Fishhopper Restaurant. It is heavily overgrown with marine life and is easily mistaken for a rock.

Hopkins Reef

Have you ever thought about diving in a school? No, I'm not talking about being at one with the fish. I'm talking about a real school with laboratories and class rooms. Well, if you've ever dived at Hopkins Reef, that is exactly what you have done.

Hopkins Reef sits between the Monterey Bay Aquarium and Lover's Point on Monterey Peninsula. The area is a natural classroom and laboratory under the auspices of Stanford University's Hopkins Marine Station. Here students and professors have the opportunity to learn about the ocean and its inhabitants and to push back the frontiers of understanding with their underwater experiments.

Hopkins Reef is simply a wonderfully relaxing

place to dive. The diving area is well protected due to the presence of the rocky projections of Point Cabrillo. This Point protects the dive site from all but the worst of California's weather. The inshore area is a patch reef system with large granite outcroppings interspersed along a sandy bottom. As one gets deeper the bottom drops away in granite steps to 60 feet in the reserve and then to over 90 feet beyond, sometimes called Hopkins Deep Reef.

In the absence of human predation the fish here have grown accustomed to diving with researchers and other non-threatening divers; consequently, this is a great place for fish watching and for fish portraiture. Large lingcod and cabezon seem oblivious to the presence of divers. Some lings seem to take great pride in making divers swim around them, while others appear to chuckle at a diver's frustration at only being able to look and not kill. Yes, the fish know they are in a reserve.

Beyond the fish life is a great assortment of invertebrate life to look at and photograph. The thick covering of coralline algae and the holdfasts of giant kelp provide shelter to a great many crawly things. Nudibranchs of any color and shape may be found in plain view, while an assortment of crabs and shrimp hide in crevices in the rocks or among the encrusting algae.

The rocks of Point Cabrillo are a haul-out site for a large group of harbor seals. These playful animals will often choose to swim with divers, and it is a special moment indeed to peer around a rock and have fuzzy face peer back. Sea otters also reside here.

Access, Entry, and Hazards: This is a boat dive-only site, and a reserve (see the "Summary of Monterey's Diving Regulations" section in the introduction chapter of this book). Divers should watch for boat traffic and thick kelp.

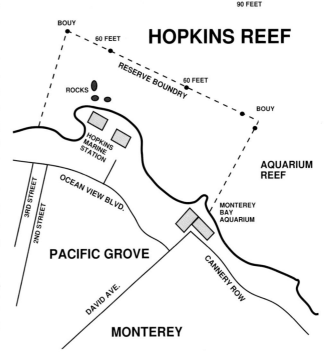

Diving With Harbor Seals

On one of my first California dives I was with a group of friends when something yanked the regulator from my mouth. Reaching back to the tank valve and following the hose back to the end, I quickly restored my air supply and began to search for the culprit. With nothing in sight, the problem was written off to an overly aggressive piece of kelp as I hurried to catch up with my friends. Two kicks later something grabbed a fin and began to pull me backwards through the water! It quickly let go and after regaining my composure, I again began to turn slowly and cautiously around. Whatever it was had long since vanished and I must have been the most paranoid diver in the sea, half expecting to meet "Jaws" around each corner. After kicking along a little further, it returned, and began to chew on the top of my new snorkel. This time I spun quickly around and met my nemesis nose to nose. It was a harbor seal and it darted off in a blink of an eye. I am not sure which has more fun in a seal-diver interaction; but it is always clear who has the upper hand.

Of all the marine mammals in Monterey, harbor seals seem to be the most friendly and frequently choose to approach divers. And, although they are great fun to watch underwater, don't do anything dumb around them like spearfishing: they will almost always get your catch. (But: it is illegal to deliberately feed a marine mammal.) Also, do not chase any marine mammal to take a photograph: let them come to you.

The seals and sea lions are referred to in scientific terms as pinnipeds, which means "fin feet." Seals and sea lions are often confused but are easily distinguished with a little practice. Sea lions belong to the family *Otariidae* and have a small external ear and are sometimes referred to as eared seals. But true seals, of the family Phocidae lack an external ear. A seal in the water will submerge by backing down, while a sea lion will propel itself down nose first. Sea lions use their large and powerful fore flippers for propulsion through the water, and seals will use their hind flippers. Sea lions have hind flippers which may be turned forward and in combination with their strong fore flippers allows them to walk or waddle on land. The hind flippers of seals cannot be turned forward and they move on land with an awkward, worm-like motion.

Harbor seals feed on octopus, squid, shellfish and small fish and usually hunt in the early morning hours. They then spend the rest of the day sleeping on offshore rocks. They are promiscuous in their breeding behavior and do not form harems as do sea lions. Pupping occurs in March through May on isolated beaches throughout the state and the newborns are capable of swimming from birth. The mother only cares for the young seal for a few weeks and will often leave the pup alone on the beach for an hour or so while she is hunting. Good-intentioned beachcombers often rescue these "abandoned" seals. It's best to leave them untouched and allow the mother to reclaim its pup.

Harbor seal.

Lover's Point

Lover's Point is located on Ocean View Boulevard within the city limits of Pacific Grove, about half way between the Monterey Bay Aquarium and Point Pinos. This is a particularly convenient place to dive since you can park close to the water and enjoy interesting diving close to shore. This is one of those sites where unusual things can almost be expected to happen.

On the east side of the point are two small sand beaches with easy access via stone stairs. These are very well protected from the swell, regardless of direction and, consequently, are popular places to take beginner scuba students on their first check-out dive.

California scorpionfish.

The sand beach gives way to eel grass-covered rocky ledges in four to eight feet of water that drop away to a flat rock and sand bottom. A little farther offshore the predominantly sand bottom is dotted with rocky pinnacles that stretch up 10 to 20 feet from the 30-to 40-foot bottom.

On these pinnacles can be found a cornucopia of colorful invertebrate life. Dense colonies of dime-sized strawberry anemones carpet the rocks is in hues of red, orange, and lavender. Larger anemones such as the red rose, spotted rose, or giant green dot the rocky surfaces and surge channels.

Within the nooks and crannies of the pinnacles hide an assortment of fish. The fish here offer a varied contrast for the underwater photographer with both the beautifully ornamented snubnose sculpins and the grotesque monkeyface-eel. The latter is not an eel at all but is a member of the prickleback family and is more closely related to the blennies than true eels. They hide in holes during the day and only venture out at night to feed on algae. Medium-to-small game fish including rockfish, cabezon, and lingcod find homes here. Although some divers spearfish here, there are better places within the bay for game hunting.

Bat rays are commonly found on the sand bottom to the east of the tip of Lover's Point. These stingrays are the only members of the eagle ray family in California and feed on clams and other mollusks. They will swim along the bottom until they detect the stream of water from the exhaust siphon of a clam, will then settle on the sand bottom and excavate a three-to four-foot-in-diameter hole by flapping their pectoral fins. These rays have strong, flat teeth capable of crushing the strongest clam shell. Their Latin name, which translates to "grinder ray," was given to them because of their eating habits and teeth.

At times, 20 or more feeding bat rays can be found within a small area. Once they have their holes dug and are busy feeding they can be very reluctant to leave. If slowly approached divers can get almost to within touching distance before the rays bolt away. Once one ray is spooked all of the nearby rays depart in a frenzied rush under cover of a great cloud of sand.

The west side of the point is more exposed to the ocean swell, and is normally rougher and more surgey that the more protected side. Consequently, it gets less diver traffic, and there is a greater chance of seeing larger marine animals. Here divers may find large torpedo rays and shovel-

ROCK AND SAND

BAT RAYS

EEL GRASS

SAND

BEACH

PARKING

LOVER'S POINT

OCEAN VIEW BLVD.

RESTROOM

PARK

RESTAURANT

STAIRS

BEACH

PIER

STAIRS

PARKING

BEACH

OCEAN VIEW BLVD.

Treefish.

Bat stars.

nose guitarfish. The former can deliver a powerful jolt of electricity and are in the look-but-don't-touch category, while the latter are quite harmless, even though they can be much larger.

The topography here is somewhat similar to the east side but is more rocky and there is a denser kelp bed. The bottom gradually drops away from 20 feet to about 70 feet over about 200 yards, and good diving begins only about 50 yards from shore. The area has a mostly sandy bottom with some rocky ledges. Out of the sand jut massive pinnacles that are covered with a healthy growth of encrusting invertebrates, which are colorful areas for macro photography. Divers should plan their dive and reserve enough air to navigate beneath the kelp that can be very thick in the summer months.

Lover's point is a great place for a night dive. Octopus may be found in great numbers along with monkeyface-eels, and an occasional wolf-eel. This is a particularly easy night dive to plan because of the well-lit parking lot and access.

Access, Entry, and Hazards: Divers may park in the metered lot at either side of the Park. Access is via stone steps on either side of the Point. Lover's Point carries various restrictions as to when you can dive and where, and is within the Pacific Grove Marine Gardens Fish Refuge (see the "Summary of Monterey's Diving Regulations" section in the introduction chapter of this book). Divers should watch for boat traffic and surge, particularly on the west entry.

Diving with Octopuses

Lover's Point is a good spot to observe octopus. These shell-less mollusks are normally thought of as being children of the night and remain hidden away inside their dens until after the sun sets. Often their dens may be identified by the pile of refuse directly outside. Octopus in Northern California feed primarily on snails, clams, crabs, and shrimp, and discard their inedible leftovers on their front door step. The predominant octopus in Northern California is the red octopus which grows to about 10 inches from tentacle tip to tentacle tip.

Lover's Point is one of the few places that I know of where octopuses may be consistently found during the day. Look for them on the sand bottom between rocks or up on the kelp itself. Sometimes they may be seen swimming through the mid-water in a behavioral pattern that is more squid-like than octopus-like. I am not certain why octopus here venture into the open during the day, but I suspect that this habitat supports a larger-than-average population and that the thick kelp bed above limits the amount of sunlight penetration.

Octopuses have the ability to change color very rapidly due to the presence of specialized cells in their skin called chromatophores. An octopus can contract and expand these

cells and selectively expose or hide pigment granules within the chromatophores. In this way the animal can change from black to bright red to white and then to a sand-like mottled pattern in a matter of seconds. Some of this expression of color reflects the emotional state of the animal, and at other times it will select a color and texture to blend in with its surroundings.

Otter Cove

The Otter Cove parking area is only a few minutes from Downtown Monterey and receives so little diver attention that you'll think that you've driven for hours to escape the crowds. This entry is about halfway between the more calmer dive locations in Monterey Bay and the generally more rugged Point Pinos. This spot has more game and marine life than calmer, more heavily dived spots.

The water near shore is shallow and consists of a boulder-strewn bottom. The shallow water goes a long way out: 50-75 feet offshore you can still stand up. These rocks are covered with algae and are quite slippery. Divers should exercise caution, particularly at low tide when crossing these rocks.

At about 150 yards out the bottom drops away quickly to 50 feet. Here the bottom is sandy with massive rocky pinnacles, and these rocks support a thick bed of kelp during the summer and fall months. Divers should reserve enough air to return under, rather than through, the kelp canopy.

These pinnacles are covered with a colorful growth of invertebrates. Huge red *Telia* anemones dot the surfaces of the surge channels, and giant green anemones are more common in calmer water where sunlight reaches the bottom. Some pinnacles are covered with thick carpets of strawberry anemones, while others are covered with yellow, orange or cobalt encrusting sponges. Huge patches of some rocks are covered with bryozoans, and numerous species of nudibranch are seen grazing on the encrusting invertebrates.

Small lingcod and cabezon are often found hiding in rocky nooks and crannies. These are ambush predators and sit patiently for a crab or octopus or juvenile rockfish to wander too close. Numerous species of rockfish are also found here: gopher, blue, brown, and the occasional vermilion. Small non-game fish such as sculpins, kelpfish, and gobys can be seen fluttering from rock to rock.

If you veer to the right as you head out from the beach the bottom is mostly sand with a few rocky areas. The kelp here is particularly thin and makes for an easy traverse in summer. Look for bat rays on the sandy bottom.

Access, Entry, and Hazards: This prime entry point sits at the intersection of Ocean View Boulevard and Siren Street in Pacific Grove. Walk down the new stone stairway to the short, sandy beach. On calm days the waist-deep water is easy to traverse, but should be avoided on rough days. When the strong northwesterly swell is up, the waves can wrap around Point Pinos quite effectively. The western point of Otter Cove is used by surfers on rough days. That should give you an idea of how ugly it can get. Divers should watch for boat traffic. Otter Cove is within the Pacific Grove Marine Gardens Fish Refuge (see the "Summary of Monterey's Diving Regulations" section in the introduction chapter of this book).

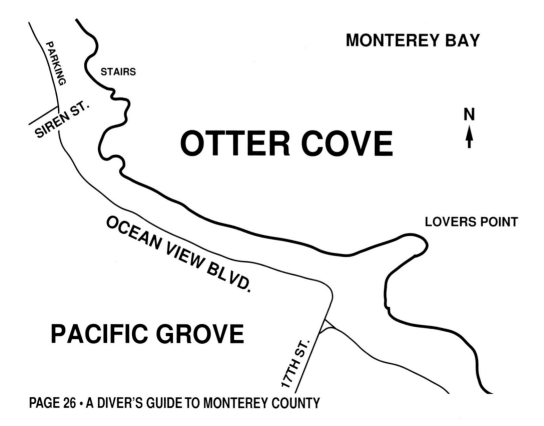

Diving with Sea Otters

One of the big attractions of Otter Cove is, of course, the sea otters. The cute and fuzzy critters are always seen here and 15 to 20 animals are normally found sunning themselves in a group at the far edge of the main kelp bed.

Otters eat continuously. Unlike other marine mammals they lack an insulating layer of fat, and rely on consuming massive quantities of food each day to maintain their body temperature. They also sport one of the finest fur coats of any animal. It was this fur coat that almost resulted in the otter's extinction. Today's California otter has multiplied from a small group located off of Big Sur in the 1930s to now total over 2000 animals.

Otters feed on clams, abalone, urchins, fat innkeeper worms, and other invertebrates. Much of their foraging occurs in sandy bottoms where they dig substantial holes to get at the clams and fat innkeeper worms. Of course they prefer abalone and urchins, but these are getting harder to come by. These fuzzy mammals are tool users and each animal has its preferred tool to bash open clam and abalone shells. Some prefer rocks, and others prefer discarded soda bottles. One man's trash may be an otter's tool!

The otter has dramatically changed the marine environment since its repopulation occurred. Urchins and abalone are normally very difficult to find in otter country. These invertebrates are the principal predators of kelp. As a result of the predation by otters the kelp beds are now considerably thicker.

Otters are great fun to dive with. They are normally more shy than seals or sea lions but occasionally choose to approach divers. Often, I see otters taking a nap on a diver's surf mat, and are sometimes very reluctant to give the diver his mat back.

Divers can often surprise an otter as they dig out shellfish in a sandy bottom. However, otters have been known to swim right up to divers and crawl on top of the diver's head. I've been told that they are particularly fond of video cameras.

Coral Street

Coral Street is one of those sites that you would like to dive every day, but its unprotected location means you can only get in when the ocean is very calm. There is a small point to the west, providing moderate protection from a westerly swell, but the small cove is often washed out in a northwesterly wind and swell.

The inshore bottom is comprised of rocky boulders covered with palm kelp and, in a little deeper water, coralline algae. The bottom is shallow for some distance, so divers normally follow the channel running down the center of the cove to get to deeper water and to avoid crawling over the rocks at low tide.

A bit further out the bottom consists of a sawtooth pattern of ridges and channels that run parallel to shore. Initially, the tops of the ridges are in about 10 feet of water and the bottoms in 15. As the depth increases the ridge tops come up to about 20 feet and the bottoms to 30 feet. After one swims a little over 200 yards, the ridges fall away to a sand-and-rocky-pinnacle bottom with a maximum depth of 60 feet. There are numerous abalone and rock scallops way back in crevices. These are protected by law, so look but don't touch.

Rocks are covered more with algae than encrusting invertebrates. Several species of brown algae and thick carpets of red, coralline algae cover all of the rocks. The more abundant invertebrate life is found in deeper water: colorful nudibranchs, sea cucumbers, and sponges. The water is clearer here than most Monterey sites, and underwater photographers will enjoy capturing the rocky walls and canyons with clear water and ample light.

Spearfishers will be reasonably happy with the assortment of rockfish and cabezon found here. Often El Niño brings up warm water fish such as sheephead up from Southern California. Serious hunters will do better if they bring a kayak for access to deeper water and more fish. This is a good spot to find monkeyface-eels back in holes.

Access, Entry, and Hazards: Divers may park on Ocean View Boulevard and walk down a short, stone staircase to a rock and gravel beach. On calm days the beach is free of surf, and entries and exits are fairly easy. There may be a strong current offshore and the surf can come up here rather quickly. This site is within the Pacific Grove Marine Gardens Fish Refuge (see the "Summary of Monterey's Diving Regulations" section in the introduction chapter of this book).

Chase Reef

Chase Reef is the most northerly dive site in the Monterey Peninsula. This reef is directly exposed to unattenuated ocean swell and is continually swept by ocean currents. The rich, nutrient-laden waters here support some of the most prolific marine life in Monterey Bay.

This rocky reef is actually composed of two reef structures. The inner reef begins between 200 and 300 yards offshore and left from Coral Street Beach. The reef runs parallel to shore and consists of a series of rocky ledges and pinnacles that drops from 30 feet to a sand bottom in 50-60 feet of water. The visibility on the reef is the very best in the Monterey area on any given day, running 20-30 feet on bad days and frequently getting up to 60-70 feet during the fall and winter months. Because of the distance from shore, most diving here is done from a boat.

The reef is easy to locate because of the thick growth of giant kelp that clearly outlines the reef, except during the winter months. The top of the reef supports a heavy growth of palm kelp providing a canopy for royal carpets of strawberry anemones a bit lower on the rocks.

The outer reef is located a little farther offshore in deeper water (40-110 feet) and runs to Point Pinos. The structure of the outer reef is more highly textured than the inner, with huge pinnacles, deep canyons, and large arches. Some of the arches are big enough to swim through. The deeper rock walls are decorated with Metridium and giant rose anemones. The combination of sheer walls and large, colorful anemones make this an excellent spot for wide-angle photography.

Chase Reef is also noted for its large population of lingcod, cabezon, and assorted species of rockfish. Lingcod are normally found back in holes, so a dive light is handy, while cabezon and rockfish are normally found in the open. Often huge schools of blue rockfish, as well as schools of bait fish, will move through the kelp bed. The combination of fish, green kelp, blue water, and sunlight streaming in from behind, makes a very pretty picture.

Due to the extreme exposure of these reefs divers will find many unusual creatures here. One of these is the white-lined dirona, a nudibranch that, with its plate-like covering, looks more like an armadillo than a nudibranch. There are also an assortment of puff-ball sponges and tiny crabs and shrimp to delight the most demanding macro photographer.

In the late winter and early spring, gray whales move through the area on their northern migration. April is a particularly good month for viewing these large mammals on the way to a dive site. I have had full-grown whales breach just a few feet from an anchored inflatable, an awesome sight. Please note that is it illegal to chase or otherwise harass whales or any other marine mammal. If a mammal encounter is to occur, it is strictly up to the marine mammal.

Access, Entry, and Hazards: Most divers get to Chase Reef on one of the many Monterey charter boats, although those who own their own boats may launch from the free ramp at the Monterey breakwater. Because of its proximity to the open ocean, Chase Reef is not diveable every day of the year. When the big storm rollers come into Monterey, this is a good area to avoid, but on flat days it offers some of the best diving in Monterey Bay. Divers should watch for currents and boat traffic.

Giant kelp.

Blue rockfish.

Point Pinos

At the very tip of Monterey Bay divers find Point Pinos. Over the years this point has proven itself to be treacherous to shipping, and the point is marked with both a buoy and a lighthouse. These are needed since many ships have come to rest on the jagged offshore rocks. These include the *Frank H. Buck* on May 3, 1924.

On calm days divers with boats may anchor near the far northern point of the kelp bed, head to the bottom and follow the reef structure north. The thin kelp bed provides shelter for a diverse population of fish and invertebrates.

Should you leave the kelp bed and follow a rocky finger that heads roughly north you'll find a colorful assortment of invertebrate life. The rock is honeycombed with many small cracks and holes in 90-110 feet of water. This is a good spot to photograph species of nudibranchs that are relatively uncommon on inshore reefs, and the area is good for spearfishing lingcod and rockfish. In over 100 feet of water lies the biggest bed of rock scallops in the bay. If you're looking for scallops this is the place.

Shore divers will find that they'll have to navigate through a bit of shallow water to reach a rocky bottom. The bottom falls away in a series of giant steps from 40 feet to well over 100 feet. Divers will find a highly textured bottom with giant granite boulders, caves and valleys.

Access, Entry and Hazards:
Point Pinos is best dived on calm days from a boat. Because commercial charter boats tend to head south to Carmel Bay on calm days and rarely visit this spot, the game diving here is quite good. On very calm days advanced divers may enter from either the east or west side of the point, depending on the direction of the swell. The surf can pick up quickly here, and the point offers no protection from the wind and swell. Dive here on only the calmest of days. Divers should watch for currents, thick kelp, and boat traffic.

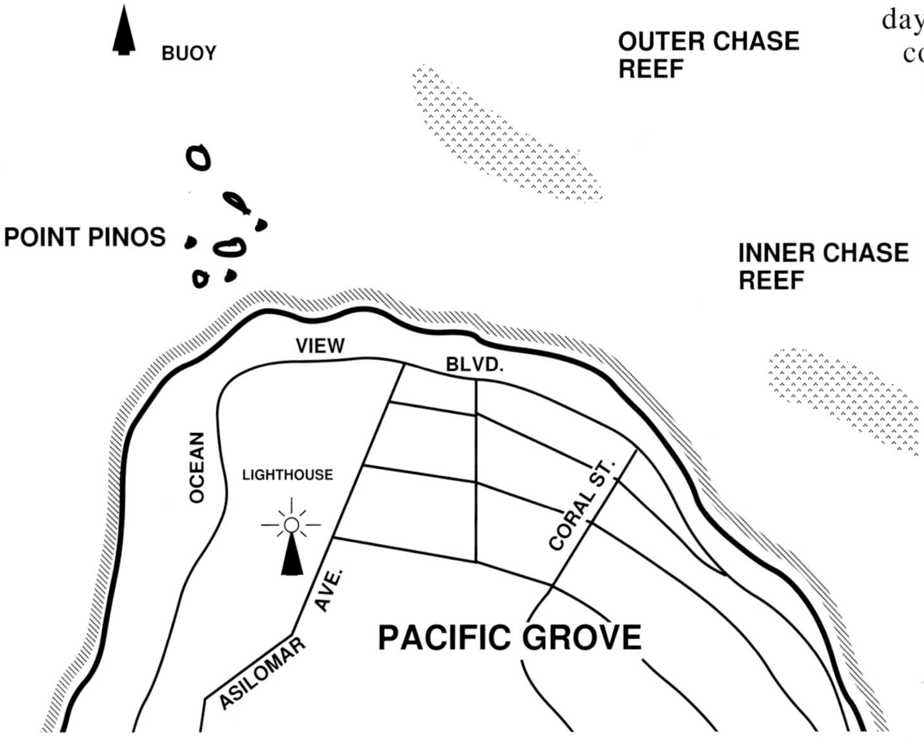

Rose anemone.

BUOY

OUTER CHASE REEF

POINT PINOS

INNER CHASE REEF

VIEW BLVD.

OCEAN

LIGHTHOUSE

CORAL ST.

ASILOMAR AVE.

PACIFIC GROVE

Monterey Shipwrecks

As one rounds Point Pinos from Monterey Bay, the personality of the ocean changes quite dramatically. Divers on boats heading from the breakwater around into Carmel Bay always notice they have arrived at Point Pinos because here is where you must hold on to keep from being knocked over. From Point Pinos to Cypress Point is a wild and untamed stretch of coastline with no easy entries. All of the sites described in this section are difficult dives. Gone are the calm beaches and protected dive entries. Dives here are not fun and relaxing; they are, however, very exciting. Few divers venture into these rough waters, and most of those who do are looking for shipwrecks and big animals.

It seems that old ships never rust away in ports, they are pushed by their owners 'till they are taken by the sea. And they almost never go down in nice places to dive. They mostly end up on rocky, jagged headlands that are pounded by wind and surf. This is the nature of the coastline between Point Pinos and Cypress Point.

Up until quite recently the only way to move people and cargo up and down the coast of California was by ship. It was not until 1876 that rail service was available from San Francisco to Los Angeles, and it would not be until 1937 that Highway 1 between San Simeon and Carmel would open. Four hundred years of shipping has left quite a few shipwrecks to explore.

Divers may at first be disappointed by Monterey's wrecks. They are not the intact wrecks often seen in magazines where divers may view the ship as it once sailed. Rather these ships often went down near shore, and the action of wind and waves tore them to pieces. Monterey wreck diving consists of looking for artifacts. Remember, however, California law prohibits the taking of any artifacts from shipwreck sites (see the "Summary of Monterey's Diving Regulations" section in the introduction chapter of this book).

The wooden parts of all the most modern of wrecks has long since disappeared. Iron tends to corrode into a rusty mass that archeologists call concretion. What remains of these old wrecks is ceramics, precious metals (if there were any on board), and brass. In the 1800s brass was cheaper to manufacture than iron and was used heavily on ships. It is a soft metal and was not applicable to certain boiler and engine parts, but was used elsewhere wherever possible. The search for this brass is what makes wreck diving exciting.

Access, Entry, and Hazards: Park in the 17-Mile Drive lot described; each entry is near the parking area. Divers may launch kayaks from any of these beaches or may motor their own boat down from the breakwater or launch at Stillwater Cove. Beach divers should be aware of hidden rocks, big and quickly changing surf and currents. These are all advanced sites!

Moss Cove

Just south of Point Pinos and Asilomar State Beach and Conference Grounds is Moss Beach. This wide sandy beach is the first stop on the 17-Mile Drive if you enter from the Pacific Grove Gate and is a great place to picnic, play frisbee, and sunbathe. The principally sand bottom would not lead many to dive here except for the presence of two shipwrecks.

CG 256

Prior to the development of radar and ground satellite navigation, navigation was more of an art than a science. Ships were forced to guess their position by "dead reckoning"; that is, they assumed that they were heading in a straight line as determined by the ship's compass and presumed to know their speed. They were often wrong and wind and currents threw their course off a bit. These misjudgements in the ships' positions often led to fatal mishaps.

In September of 1933 the *Coast Guard Ship #256* was sent to Monterey to "observe the sardine strike situation." Perhaps more precisely they were to be a symbol of government presence to prevent violence among the disgruntled fishermen.

The *CG 256* was a prohibition-era, 75-foot-long "rum chaser" operated by the Coast Guard. In 1933, after only one week in the Monterey area, she simply ran aground in a heavy fog just south of Asilomar State Beach. Within three days the sea broke the wooden-hulled cutter in half and then turned it to splinters.

The remains of the ship sit off the eastern point of Moss Beach, along the 17-Mile Drive in Pebble Beach. The area is mostly a sand bottom, so pieces of the wreck become ex-

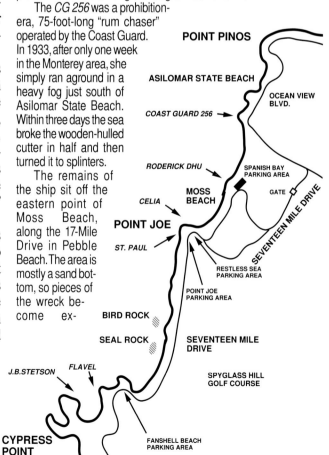

posed and covered with sand as storms and swell move the sand around. Divers commonly find brass nails that were used to fasten copper sheets to the outer hull along with assorted hardware. At low tide the ship's ribs are sometimes visible. The wreckage is easily located by parking in the "Spanish Bay" parking area and walking 100 yards or so to the rocky point to the right. Enter to the left of the point and the wreckage is found in 5 to 20 feet of water right off the point.

Roderick Dhu

The *Roderick Dhu* was christened in England in 1873 as a 1,534 ton bark. As steamers became common on the world's seas, she was reduced to serve as an oil barge and was towed up and down the California coast. In the wee morning hours the tugboat *Relief* was towing the *Roderick Dhu* toward Monterey and mistook Point Joe for the entrance to Monterey Bay. The tug got away safely from the incident, but the barge met her end on the rocks at the middle of Moss Beach. Divers can find a bit of wreckage in the shallow water. Park in the "Spanish Bay" lot at the intersection of Spanish Bay Road and the 17-Mile Drive. The wreck is located just offshore from the rocky area near the parking area.

Point Joe

This rugged point has two parking areas and two wrecks. This is an exposed area so beach entries can be a bit tricky. Watch the surf before choosing to get wet. The bottom offshore is pretty with interesting rock formations and lots of kelp and invertebrates. This is a good spot for spearfishing for rockfish.

SS Celia

Another wreck that resulted from faulty navigation was the *Celia*. On August 28,1906, the *Celia* headed south out of Santa Cruz with a load of 160,000 feet of lumber intended for Monterey. She overshot her port in the dead of night and wound up on the rocks off Point Joe.

Divers interested in visiting the wreck site should park in the "Restless Sea" parking lot on the 17-Mile Drive. Enter at the cut in the rocks near the center of the parking area and swim to the rock that is visible at low tide about 100 yards offshore and a bit to the left of the entry point. Around the wash rock divers will find the steam engine, boiler, and various pieces of brass hardware in 25 to 30 feet of water.

St. Paul

The *St. Paul* was built in Philadelphia in 1875 and was one of the few steel-hulled vessels to be wrecked in diveable depths in Monterey county. She was 197 feet long and 31 feet wide and grossed 889 tons. On August 8, 1896, she steamed out of San Simeon with a cargo of sheep and calves and headed north to Monterey. She never delivered her cargo. At 11:15 p.m. she slammed into Point Joe in a thick fog. Quick to the rescue, the crew of the *Gipsy* responded and saved not only the crew of the *St. Paul* but most of the livestock as well. The *Gipsy* was wrecked nine years later in Monterey (see earlier story).

The wreckage of the *St. Paul* lies directly off the "Point Joe" turnout on the 17-Mile Drive. Divers should enter the water through the steep-sided gap between two large rocks in the center of the parking area. The wreckage is straight out from the gap and about 100 yards offshore. There you will find a jungle gym of steel and brass rods. Among the rods are metal wheels, the propeller, and assorted brass artifacts. This is a dangerous place to dive in moderate surf.

Cypress Point

This spot is worth visiting even if you're not interested in wreck diving. The bottom here is covered with rocky pinnacles and sand channels in 20 to 70 feet of water. The rocks here experience a great deal of current and have accumulated a thick invertebrate growth that is unlike anything you will see along the Monterey/Carmel Bays. Unusual sponges, nudibranchs, and gorgonia may be found here. This is also a good spot for whale watching.

SS Flavel

The wooden-hulled *Flavel* was built in Eureka in 1917 and the 967-ton vessel carried lumber down the coast of California for only five years before she met her end. Just past midnight on December 14, 1923, the ship rammed into Cypress Point on a dark, foggy night. Captain Johnson realized that she was stuck hard on the rocks and breaking up, so he gave orders to abandon ship.

Access to Cypress Point and the wreck site is best made by boat. However, divers can enter off the rocks by crossing the 15th Tee of the Cypress Point Golf Course, or launch a kayak from Fanshell Beach. This area is closed from mid-March to mid-June due to the presence of pupping harbor seals. Park at the "Tidewater Cove Turnout." The wreckage is on the west side of the finger-like projection just on the opposite side of the Tee from the parking area. Much brass and an anchor may be found here.

SS J.B. Stetson

The *J.B Stetson* was a wooden-hulled steamer that grossed 922 tons. On her last voyage she left the Port of San Pedro and headed, mostly empty, to pick up 300 tons of cargo waiting for her in Monterey. She never arrived. At 1:00 a.m. on the night of September 3, 1934, Cypress Point claimed another ship. The *Stetson* was slowly plying through the "worst fog they had ever seen," when she ran aground at Cypress Point. This was about 150 yards west of the resting place of the *Flavel* and 11 years later.

Today the wreckage sits in 20 to 25 feet of water just off Cypress Point. There is an anchor in plain view right off one rock finger, and this wreck still has a lot of brass lying about in shallow water (see map).

● BOUY

CYPRESS POINT

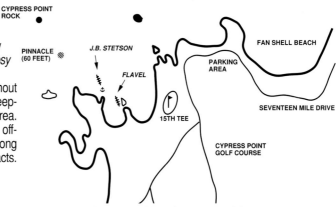

Introduction to Carmel Bay

As one rounds Cypress Point the coastline takes a distinctive cut eastward. This is the beginning of Carmel Bay, a diving area with a wide variety of experiences. This protected bay has enjoyed a rich history of fishing, farming, mining, and shipping.

During the Spanish Period the Carmel Mission was established, and over 3,000 Indians are buried in the mission's cemetery. The Spanish also gave us the Carmelite Monastery, which overlooks what we now call Monastery Beach. Pebble Beach became a Chinese fishing village in 1868, and the Del Monte Lodge was constructed in 1919. That same year Del Monte Forest was purchased by Samuel Morse, the grandnephew of the inventor of the Morse code. Samuel subdivided the forest and was careful to preserve the stands of Monterey pine and cypress trees. Today, the Del Monte Forest is a private community managed by the Pebble Beach Company.

The first three dive sites described this section are all along beautiful and rugged 17-Mile Drive. Two are boat dives only and one is a beach dive. The Pebble Beach Company has granted some beach access to the public, mostly described in the previous section. However, there is a single public beach access on the Carmel Bay side of Pebble Beach at the Beach Club (Stillwater Cove) near the Lodge at Pebble Beach. From this boat launch divers have rapid access to most of Carmel Bay.

From Pescadero Point southwards run a series of sandy beaches with good public access. These are intermediate-to-advanced dives and give the beach diver convenient access to good, near-shore diving. Sites like the Copper Roof House and

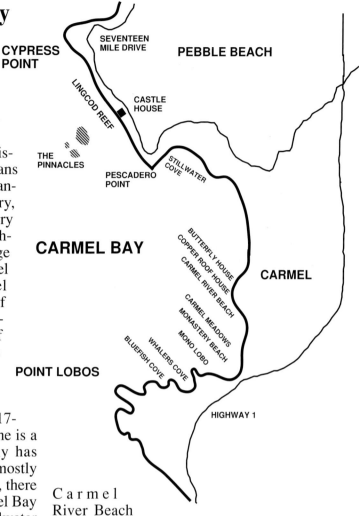

Carmel River Beach are gateways to good fishing and photography while the steep Monastery and Carmel Meadows beaches give shore divers the only access to deep waters in Northern/Central California. Of course, Carmel Bay is frequented by Monterey's charter boats, should you wish to avoid the beach entries.

Farther along the bay are the Mono-Lobo Wall and the famed Point Lobos State Reserve. This reserve has been called the "greatest meeting of land and sea" and has breathtaking scenery both above and below the water. The reserve limits access to and protects the landscape as it was before the arrival of humans.

Carmel Bay is, in general, not as well protected as Monterey Bay, so the sites are least often visited and offers a greater abundance of marine life. There is a greater sense of exploration and adventure here, where hunters will find more game. Much of Carmel Bay is part of one of two reserves/preserves. These restrict the taking of invertebrates throughout all but the first two sites mentioned, although spearfishing is only regulated in the Point Lobos Reserve.

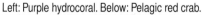

Left: Purple hydrocoral. Below: Pelagic red crab.

Lingcod Reef

Lingcod Reef is a mile-long stretch of rocky reef along Pebble Beach's 17-Mile Drive. The reef begins at Sunset Point and stretches southeast to Pescadero Point. This is a picturesque part of Monterey County where the wave-carved granite cliffs and cypress-covered hills overlook the dive sites. Famous landmarks such as the Lone Cypress and the Castle House mark boat anchorages.

CARMEL BAY

Overall, the topography of Lingcod Reef is a gently sloping rock-and-sand bottom that begins in about 20 feet and gradually drops to 60 feet. Tracks of sand wind through patch reefs, massive granite boulders, and sheer-sided pinnacles. Healthy beds of *Macrocystis* (giant kelp) cover the surface and mark the rocky areas. The topography here lends itself to exploring and makes a perfect backdrop for wide-angle photography.

These rocky reefs are covered with just about every hue of the rainbow—red *Tealia* anemones; red and lavender corynactis; yellow, orange and cobalt sponges. There is color everywhere. Amongst the cover of invertebrates hide a menagerie of crawly things. Every rock is home to some wonderful little critter to behold and to photograph. Nudibranchs from each of the four suborders are represented here with common sightings of the gaudy *Hermissenda* and *Phidiana* nudibranchs.

The fish life here is varied and impressive. Monkeyface-eels are common in small holes at the bases of rock piles, and an assortment of sculpins and greenlings hide amongst the algae and encrusting invertebrates. Healthy schools of rockfish glide through the kelp beds and well-camouflaged cabezons sulk on the bottom. Spearfishing along Lingcod Reef is about as good as it gets in Monterey/Carmel Bays. Of course, the most popular fish here is the lingcod.

Lingcod Reef has many anchorages and dive sites. Sunset Point marks the northern point of Lingcod Cove and is a good place for spearfishing. It is a bit more protected than the rest of the reef in the presence of a moderate swell. Offshore of Castle House are a number of underwater arches, some big enough to drive a small car through, while others may be used to frame divers for underwater portraits. Sightseers and photographers will find Lingcod Reef a comfortable and enjoyable dive with plenty of interesting critters to observe and photograph.

Access, Entry, and Hazards: Lingcod Reef is a boat-only site. Private boats may be launched at the Monterey Breakwater for the 30-to 60- minute ride to the site. Alternatively, it is an easy paddle by dive board or short run by inflatable from the Pebble Beach Club House Pier (restrictions apply; see the "Summary of Monterey's Diving Regulations" section in the introduction chapter of this book).

The Pinnacles

Among the best sites available to Northern California divers is Monterey's Ocean Pinnacles, or simply the Pinnacles. Located about three-quarters of a mile offshore between Pescadero Point and Cypress Point in Carmel Bay, the Pinnacles lie directly off 17-Mile Drive. The beautiful scenery of the rugged coastline, expensive mansions, and expansive golf courses are second only to the area's underwater beauty.

Throughout most of the year the Pinnacles may be located by finding the extensive kelp bed offshore from the large pink house with a high tower, nicknamed "The Castle House." However, after a period of winter storms there may be no kelp at all visible on the surface, and a depth finder comes in handy in locating this dive site. In a moderate swell the water can be observed to peak up over the most shallow point in the area. If the waves actually are breaking on the pinnacle it's a good sign that the diving may

Hunting for Lingcod

Lingcod are one of the most sought-after fish by California divers. They may be found along the entire state and some 10 million pounds are harvested annually. About six percent of the sport harvest is taken by spearfishers. Lingcod is the second most commonly speared fish in California, second only to a combined species of rockfish, genus *Sebastes*.

The scientific name for lings is *Ophiodon elongatus*, meaning "snake tooth." They are the largest member of the greenlings, the *Hexagrammidae* family. They should not be confused with unrelated Atlantic cod. Lingcod feed on juvenile rockfish, squid, and their favorite food, octopus. They lie in wait for unsuspecting prey to wander too close and then pounce and grab their dinner with razor sharp teeth.

Lingcod are very territorial and most fish, particularly the males, move around very little. During most of the year there is a segregation of sexes with the smaller males being found in shallow water less than 100 feet deep. The females are often in water exceeding 100 feet and often to 400 feet. Because of this depth segregation, some 70 percent of all lings taken by divers are males.

This situation changes in November through March when the females move inshore to breed. Eggs are laid in small caves or rocky depressions in 10 to 40 feet of water and are externally fertilized. Soon afterwards the female departs and leaves the male with the role of guardian. Lings are polygamists and a single ling may guard as many as four nests during the seven-week incubation period. This house-husband will aggressively protect the egg mass from predatory crabs and rockfish. Should the male be removed, the eggs will be rapidly consumed. Most divers consider it very unsportsmanlike to shoot a nest-sitting fish. Each nest contains some 500,000 eggs and shooting the male will compromise the catch in the future.

When hunting lings look in small holes and for perches on top of rocky outcroppings. Have a little patience and look carefully since the fish blend in well to their surroundings. Sometimes a flashlight is helpful to find lings back in holes; some divers attach the flashlight directly on to the end of their speargun. Should you startle a ling before you get off a shot, stick around the area. Lings are territorial and will usually return to their favorite perch rather quickly after being disturbed.

Some spearfishers have developed some clever ways to attract lings. One technique is to take the butt of your dive knife and bang it on a rock several times. If there is a ling in a nearby hole chances are he will come out to investigate all the clatter.

Another technique was developed by a friend of mine who would always take his wife diving and ask her to carry the stringer. Once a fish was speared he would regularly circle around behind her. Often he would find a big ling stalking his wife! Throughout the dive, each fish speared seemed to be bigger than the one before and some full stringers were taken by this method.

A heavy, two-banded speargun is recommend for taking big lingcod that can get up to 40 pounds or more. In the summer months when the smaller fish are inshore, a pole spear or a lighter gun will do. It is unwise to shoot a big fish with a pole spear. You'll probably end up breaking your spear, mortally wounding and losing the fish, and making a group of sea stars very happy.

Lingcod occasionally have a light green or blue color to their fillets. This color is due to their diet and in no way indicates that the fish is bad. In fact, the color always disappears on cooking.

---

be better elsewhere.

In season the kelp beds here are far thicker than you will find in most other Monterey locations. Giant kelp is the fastest growing living thing on earth, growing at the fantastic rate of over a foot and a half per day, and requires a great deal of nutrients, particularly nitrogen-containing chemicals, from the water. The Pinnacles are constantly bathed in nutrient-rich Pacific waters out of the nearby Carmel Trench, and not only the kelp beds but the communities of bottom-dwelling invertebrates explode in a kaleidoscope of life.

Diving through the kelp bed on a sunny day can be an exhilarating, almost religious experience. As the sunlight penetrates the kelp canopy it breaks up into so many sunbeams, each rotating around the center in a circular motion. The back-lit kelp takes on rich hues of green and amber. Huge schools of blue rockfish may be observed moving through the kelp bed.

There are actually two pinnacles, the inner and the outer. The inner pinnacle juts up from the 100-foot bottom to about 15 feet of the surface. The sides of the rocky, underwater mountain drop away at about a 45-degree angle and are carved out with a series of canyons and small caves. The outer pinnacle is separate from the inner and is located about one-quarter of a mile southwest. It is composed of a group of rocky plateaus that vary between 45 to 70 feet below the surface. The sides of pinnacle drop steeply away

to the 100-foot bottom, while the upper structure is highly textured with narrow channels and valleys, allowing wonderful possibilities for exploration.

One of the first things a diver notices here is that every square inch of rock is covered with a colorful carpet of invertebrate life. Life in many parts of the ocean is limited by the amount of nutrients contained in the water. This is not so here. The limit as to how much life this area can support is strictly dependent on the available space on the rocks.

Many invertebrates add color to the reef: orange puffball, red volcano, and the dark blue cobalt sponge. Large anemones dot the rocky walls and surge channels. One species common here, which is quite rare on inshore reefs, is California hydrocoral. This coral forms a branched, rock-like skeleton of calcium carbonate in shades of pink and purple and is actually a colony composed of many individual animals. Only the outer skin of the coral is alive, and as each polyp dies it is covered over by new growth. Hydrocoral is not a true coral in that the polyps do not extend past their rocky skeleton, even at night.

In addition to creatures that fix themselves more or less permanently to the rocks, there are a number that can be found crawling around. Colorful sea cucumbers and an assortment of sea stars and crabs may be found foraging along the bottom. Many species of intricate nudibranchs including Triton nudibranch, the white-lined nudibranch, and *Phidiana* nudibranchs are common to these exposed reefs.

Because this area is exposed to the open ocean many pelagic species may also be found here. Large Medusa jellyfish with their long trailing tentacles can often be found just outside of the kelp bed.

Access, Entry, and Hazards: This is a boat-only site. Because of the exposed nature of the site and the unpredictability of the weather, the pinnacles are not diveable every day. On calm days the ride out from the marina is surely worth the effort and expense. Watch for currents and boat traffic.

Upper left: Rose anemone. Left: Diver in heavy kelp.
Lower left: Purple hydrocoral. Below: Feather duster worm.

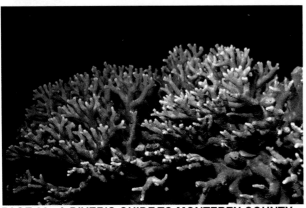

Stillwater Cove

One of the sites where I seem to spend a lot of time is Stillwater Cove in Carmel Bay. The cove is aptly named since it is one of the calmest spots on the Central California Coast. Most people dive Stillwater Cove from one of Monterey's charter dive boats. After a deep dive at the Pinnacles or Mono-Lobo Wall, the captain always looks for a calm spot in shallow water for a lunch break and a shallow second or third dive. Experience has shown that Stillwater Cove is one of the best of such sites.

Offshore, the bottom is mostly rock, dotted with massive rocks. The rock bottom gradually slopes down to about 40 feet, then abruptly drops away in a massive wall to a sand bottom in about 60 feet These rocks are covered with all of the colorful marine life that makes California diving so interesting—carpets of red corynactis anemones, giant green and blood red *Telia* anemones, yellow and cobalt blue sponges. There is an enormous growth of both giant and bull kelp, with feather boa kelp becoming more common in shallower water.

Monkeyface-eels are abundant here but often go unnoticed. Their distorted face is a bit grotesque, but nonetheless interesting to photograph. Besides interesting critters to look at there is an abundance of game fish here. Schools of blue rockfish move in and out of the kelp bed and good-sized cabezon are found in the crevices. This seems to be a better than average place to hunt for lingcod. Year around there is a good population of legal-sized and bigger male lings. These are normally found deep back in a hole. As fish go, lings are one of least intelligent and make a fairly easy target for those with a flashlight and a little patience.

The wash rocks in the center of the cove carry the name Pescadero and are a wonderful shallow-water dive when conditions are calm. In only 5-to-15 feet of water, divers find an assortment of colorful invertebrates and small fish. Pescadero Rocks is also a great place to observe and photograph nudibranchs. The simple dorids such as the lemon and Monterey nudibranch are here in abundance. Just to test your photographic skill there are also more photogenic species: the orange and white clown nudibranch, the gaudy red and white *Phidiana,* and the ostentatious *Dendronotidae.*

This cove has an abundance of hermit crabs. The winter is mating time for hermit crabs. The larger female crabs are often seen carrying around the smaller males, shell and all. She keeps him around as long as she is willing to mate and then sets him free—like a bound concubine.

Access, Entry, and Hazards: While most dive Stillwater Cove from charter boats, there is good access from shore. Small inflatable boats and dive kayaks are easily launched from the pier or beach and provide access to the entire Carmel Bay. The diving right near the pier is not so hot, so some kind of dive vehicle is recommended (restrictions apply; see the "Summary of Monterey's Diving Regulations" section in the introduction chapter of this book).

Vermillion rockfish.

Cabezon Hunting

Cabezon *(Scorpaenichthys marmoratus)* are the largest member of the *Cottidae* family (the sculpins) on the west coast and can grow to 30 inches and weigh 25 pounds. They have a typical sculpin shape with a large head, flattened mouth, and a long, tapering body. The mottled coloration of this species varies greatly between individuals, but the males generally have a red base color and the females normally have a green base. Females are also a little larger than the males. All individuals have a cirrus, a hair-like projection of skin over each eye, and are smooth skinned, having no scales.

Cabezon can be found from British Columbia to central Baja, from intertidal areas to depths of 250 feet, although they are, on the average, located at a comfortable sport diving depth of 35 feet. The larger individuals are usually found in deeper water, and this species is almost exclusively associated with rocky bottoms.

The greater part of a cabezon's day is spent perched on a rock, waiting for dinner to crawl or swim by. They are so well camouflaged that they are almost invisible.

A cabezon's diet is made up of about 50 percent crabs and the remainder divided equally between small rockfish and mollusks. At high tide, cabezon migrate into the intertidal areas to feed on limpets and small abalone. This prey is swallowed whole and, after being partially digested, the shell is regurgitated. Many of the highly polished abalone shells that divers find are a result of this creature's digestive juices.

Mating takes place beginning in October and lasts through March, with activity peaking in January. Eggs are laid in pink or green masses of 50,000 to 100,000 in rocky crevices and are externally fertilized. In this species the females quickly abandon the nest leaving the male with the role of guardian. This seems unnecessary as the eggs possess potent toxin and are rarely eaten by predators even when the males are removed from the nest. Sports-minded spearfishers never take nest-sitting fish since they are reluctant to leave their nest and are too easy to spear. The young hatch in about two weeks and are pelagic, sometimes being found several hundred miles from shore. After they grow to about one and one-half inches they begin to take on the color of the adults and settle into tide pools.

Cabezon are a very easy fish to spear. A small, single-banded speargun (otherwise known as a rock gun) or a pole spear is preferred as this species usually does not get large enough to justify anything larger. Also, it is easier to aim a smaller gun while working highly textured, rocky bottoms, and your spear is less likely to be damaged if you miss the fish and hit a rock. The most difficult task is to notice them at all before you pass on by. Stay close to the bottom and look for their eyes, which may be the only thing to distinguish them from the rock on which they are sitting. Once spotted, avoid direct eye contact as this will usually spook them. Try to aim your spear just behind the head, since the skulls of cabezon are particularly difficult to puncture. Remember, though, that the roe is very poisonous and should never be eaten.

Copper Roof House

The Copper Roof House is a landmark in Carmel for both divers and tourists. This arty little house sits right on a bluff above the ocean and offers its residences a wonderful view of Carmel Bay. It is the house's unique copper roof with its green oxidized color that gives the dive site its name.

The house sits on a little point in the middle of Carmel Bay, and this relatively exposed location provides convenient access to a healthy reef community. Offshore is a patch reef system with large rocky areas interspersed among sandy flats. The rocky areas support a thick bed of giant kelp in summer and are indicative of the abundance of life underwater. Offshore the wash rocks are home to a number of harbor seals.

Many of the shallow rocks are covered with layers of coralline algae, within which smaller critters find shelter and food. In deeper water the rocks are covered with corynactis anemones. Their fluorescent red color seemingly lights up the reef. Palm kelp may be found at the tops of pinnacles and giant kelp in deeper water wherever it can find a secure spot to attach.

Among the algae may be found an assortment of nudibranchs. In fact, this is one of the best areas for finding nudibranchs, and some grow to enormous sizes. These are of the dorid family and may be the size of your fist or bigger. The big ones are primarily lemon nudibranchs, snow white dorids, or Monterey dorids.

Within the nooks and crannies of the rocks live an assortment of critters. In some areas the cracks are chock full of abalone, mostly blacks. The cracks here are both so deep and narrow that otters can only look but not partake of these tasty critters. The area is also part of a marine reserve; divers are prohibited from taking any kind of shellfish. With all of the talk these days about otters and humans depleting shellfish resources, it's nice to see a stronghold of abalone here.

This spot receives a lot less diver traffic than nearby locations, partly because of the exposure to the swell and partly because few divers have heard of the spot. That means that the spearfishing is good. Besides good-sized cabezon, numerous lingcod may also be found. These are not the trophies that are found elsewhere, but they're big enough for dinner. The area also supports a good population of rockfish. Sometimes huge schools of blue rockfish may be found in the kelp beds. This is perfect quarry for a free diver with a pole spear.

Access, Entry, and Hazards: Divers should park their cars on Scenic Road near the intersection of Martin Avenue. The City of Carmel has refurbished the deteriorating stairs to the beach. The entire stretch of beach is diveable, but divers tend to enter the water near the stairs. Watch for thick kelp and surge.

Butterfly House

The Butterfly House is located at the corner of Scenic Road and Stewart Way in Carmel. This small cove is long and thin, with rocky reefs flanking both sides that provide considerable protection from the swell. When the northwest swell is running, the beach is one of the calmest in the entire Carmel Bay. During the spring and summer it may be the only diveable spot for several miles. However, when the south swell is up, the full force of the ocean runs straight down the mouth of the cove.

The beach has a few rocks in the surf line that need to be avoided, and then the bottom gradually drops away from 5 to 15 feet. This is a pretty area to explore if there is little swell. There is a colorful display of marine algae on the rocks and a host of small crabs, nudibranchs, and snails can be found. This area is not a lot of fun if there if any surge at all.

From the shallow rocky area the bottom drops to 40 feet to a sand bottom with few redeeming features for divers. The bottom again becomes rocky when it drops to 50 feet in the major offshore kelp bed. This is a fine example of what a kelp bed is supposed to look like—thick and forest-like. The area experiences limited currents, so the kelp stands

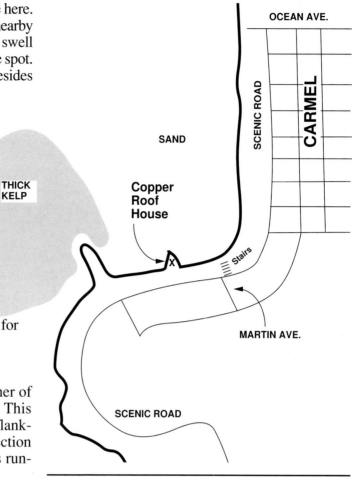

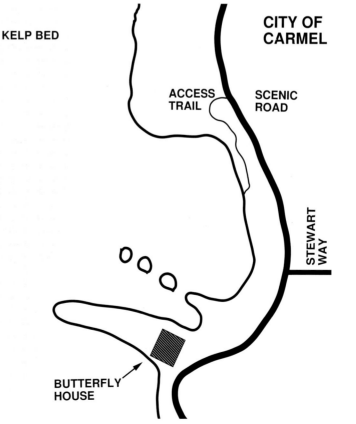

A diver observes a cabezon.

Copper rockfish.

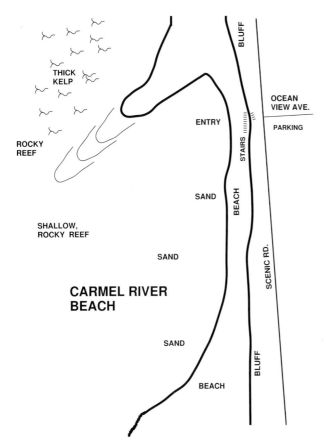

THICK KELP

ROCKY REEF

ENTRY

OCEAN VIEW AVE.

PARKING

SAND

BLUFF

STAIRS

BEACH

SHALLOW, ROCKY REEF

SAND

SCENIC RD.

CARMEL RIVER BEACH

SAND

SAND

BEACH

BLUFF

straight up like so many Grecian columns.

The bottom under the kelp is rocky with valleys, canyons, and small caves. The kelp tends to filter much of the crud from the water, and the visibility here is often better than at nearby locations. This is a good spot for wide-angle photography, particularly kelp shots. If you're lucky you might see a gray whale at Butterfly. On their northerly migration during the spring they sometimes stop by the north side of Carmel Bay.

Butterfly House gets fewer divers than other spots around, partly because of limited parking and partly because there are no facilities here. There are a few lingcod in the deeper rocky reef and a few small cabezons as well. Schools of blue rockfish are sometimes found at the outside edge of the kelp bed.

Access, Entry, and Hazards: To get to Butterfly House drive west on Rio Road, turn left on Santa Lucia, and make a left on Scenic. The site is named after the house on the east edge of a little cove with the wing-like roof. Divers need to find legal parking on the street either on Scenic Road or Stewart Way. They can then hike to the north end of the beach and along a short rocky trail that drops 20 feet to a nice sand beach. Watch for thick kelp and sometimes heavy surge.

Carmel River Beach

A bit off the beaten path site can be found at Carmel River Beach. While there may be a hundred divers across the bay at Monastery, there may be only a few divers here. There is a large, rocky reef system that protects the north end of the beach from swell from almost any direction. Entries are made near the rocks at the north end of the beach. A bit farther down the beach, the protection wanes and the steep beach combined with loose pea sand can make the entries here a bit of a challenge on rough days.

Most divers swim out around the rocky reef before submerging. Once at the near end of the kelp bed they have two choices. On the inside of the kelp bed is a rocky bottom in 20 to 30 feet of water. If the swell is pumping this area can have big surge, but can be very pretty on calm days. Thick kelp covers the surface and large boulders are strewn about the bottom. On the boulders is a healthy covering of coralline algae, and hiding among the algae are nudibranchs and small fish to delight the sightseer and photographer.

On the outside of the kelp bed the bottom drops off to 40-50 feet to a sand bottom that is dotted with many oversized pinnacles. Many jut straight up from the bottom some 20 feet or more. These create an assortment of mini-walls that are simply stunning. This is one of the few places in the Monterey area where beach divers can easily get to good, vertical walls.

The walls are covered with a bouquet of colorful sponges and anemones. Yellows, oranges, reds: there is plenty of color here, and the walls are excellent for both macro and wide-angle photography. There is a wide variety of little fish to observe: sculpins, greenlings, small rockfish, and gobys.

Carmel River Beach is a good spot for spearfishing, but not by swimming from the beach. The better fishing grounds are located around the point to the right, a bit farther than most divers would like to swim. A diver's kayak is an ideal vehicle to reach these fishing grounds as it is a short paddle, and it is easy to carry the light kayaks down the steps. Some divers actually carry small inflatable boats down the steps! The outer point is used by CenCal for their first Freediving (spearfishing) Meet each season.

Access, Entry, and Hazards: Divers should park on Ocean View Avenue at the intersection with Scenic Road and take the wooden staircase to the beach. From the top of the stairs you get a good view of the entire Carmel Bay with Point Lobos to the right and Monastery Beach to the left. Watch for thick kelp, rough entries, and surge.

Carmel Meadows

This is one of those "in between spots" between Carmel River Beach entry and Monastery Beach. The wide, sandy beach is marked by large rock outcroppings at each end. Inshore, the bottom is mostly rock with deep canyons, pinnacles, and vertical mini-walls. Various species of algae cover the rocks and stalked tunicates peek out from behind the algae. There are several arches, some big enough to swim through and others resembling portholes. This is a very nice place for exploration in only 20-40 feet of water.

The area supports a healthy bed of giant kelp. This is a good place to spearfish for lingcod, cabezon, and numerous species of rockfish. At the edge of the kelp bed are often found huge schools of blue rockfish. Leopard sharks come inshore to sandy bottoms to pup in the late winter and spring.

Beyond the kelp the bottom turns to sand and rolls away into the Carmel Trench. Divers should be careful of their depth here as you can get real deep real fast. The mostly sand bottom is quite interesting here. Huge mats of writhing brittle stars

Sunstar.

Nudibranch eggs.

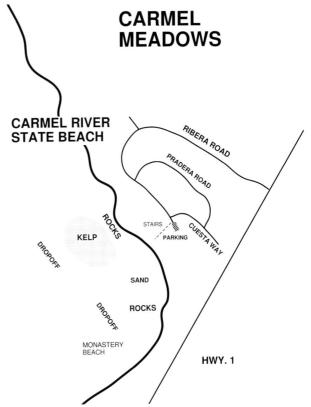

CARMEL MEADOWS

CARMEL RIVER STATE BEACH

RIBERA ROAD

PRADERA ROAD

CUESTA WAY

STAIRS

PARKING

ROCKS

KELP

DROPOFF

SAND

ROCKS

DROPOFF

MONASTERY BEACH

HWY. 1

cover the sand in some areas, while armies of olive shells march through others. There are numerous sand-dwelling anemones to be found along with their chief predator—the rainbow nudibranch. This is a good spot to photograph these animals since this site offers better visibility that sandy bottoms elsewhere.

In some areas the sand bottom is dotted with large boulders and rocks, and divers can reach extreme depth descending from one rock to another. These isolated rocky patches are a great place to hunt for gopher and brown rockfish.

Access, Entry, and Hazards: Divers should park at the intersection of Ribera Road and Cuesta Way in Carmel. Ribera Road intersects with Highway 1 between the Crossroads and Monastery Beach. There is a limited parking area, and divers must hike down eighty steps on a well-maintained stairway of railroad ties. Enter off the beach near the rocks to the right or left. The sand here is coarse like that found at Monastery, so divers should watch their footing while going in and out of the water. This is a steep beach and the plunging breakers can be dangerous on rough days. Divers should also watch their depth gauges; it can get real deep here.

The beach at Carmel Meadows.

Monastery Beach

Northern California divers are fortunate that one of the fingers of the Monterey Submarine Canyon, the Carmel Canyon or "Trench," runs almost right up to shore, and Monastery Beach is one of the few places in California where beach divers may have access to really deep water right from shore. The steep granite walls of the canyon are several thousands of feet deep in places, and divers can never view more than a small portion of this grand structure.

To find the Trench, snorkel along the southern edge of the kelp bed on the north end of the beach until you near the prominent wash rock. Submerge at this point and follow the contour of the rock bottom. If you submerge before reaching the vicinity of the wash rock, the canyon may

still be located but the bottom consists of mainly of steeply-sloping sand.

The walls of the canyon at this location slant down at over a 70-degree angle, and it is very easy to quickly get deeper than you realize. The wall consists of many large boulders and rocks, so the dive mainly consists of "boulder hopping." In the shallows the rocks are covered with an assortment of giant and palm kelp and an assortment of large anemones, both the giant green and colonies of aggregating anemones. Many boulders are covered with lush carpets of red *Corynactis* anemones.

As one drops deeper the kelp begins to thin out. The bottom life shifts to large anemones, with the rocks encrusted with orange volcano and cobalt sponges. Here is one of the best areas for spearfishing, with large lingcod and cabezon found among the nooks and crannies of the bottom, while

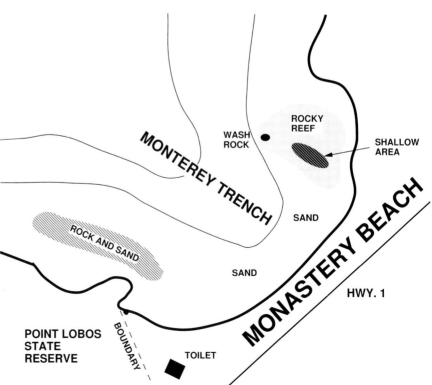

dense schools of blue rockfish cruise along the outer edge of the kelp canopy. Large Medusa jellyfish may be commonly seen here along with ocean sunfish.

As divers drop below 80 feet the rocks become encrusted with various small invertebrates, bryozoans, sea cucumbers and some sponges. Between the rocks and back in holes are an assortment of rock scallops. Although rock scallops are very tasty, divers are warned that the entire Carmel Bay is an ecological preserve from which no invertebrates may be taken.

Divers with a little more energy will want to swim around to the far side of the wash rock. The bottom there slopes gently to about 30 feet and then drops vertically—and I do mean vertically—to very great depths. The sensation was like stepping out of an airplane at 30,000 feet. The feeling of complete mobility in all dimensions is about as close as many of us will get to sprouting wings and being able to fly. The wall continues down to a large overhang at 110 feet. The overhangs sticks out about 10 feet and underneath is often a good spot for spearfishing. Once past the overhang the wall continues to head straight down. We can only speculate what lies below.

When visiting Monastery take some time to

Monastery Beach.

The "Monastery Crawl."

explore the shallow areas in addition to the trench. On the south side of the beach is a nice rock and kelp garden with an assortment of colorful invertebrates and small fish. The surf entries are normally easier at this part of the beach. Divers are treated to an assortment of little fish, shrimps, and crabs. The rocks are covered with anemones and sponges that make a nice background for photographers.

The shallow areas on the north side of the beach contain some excellent areas for macro photography and spearfishing. A great many species of nudibranchs, such as the brightly colored Spanish shawl and the horned nudibranch, as well as sea stars and sea cucumbers, inhabit the shallow area beneath the large kelp bed. This is an extraordinary place for macro photography of tunicates and flatworms.

The center of the beach is mostly sand and has the roughest wave break; it should be avoided. This beach has a reputation for having a rougher-than-average entry and exit. Divers should exercise good judgment in deciding where, and if, to enter the water here.

Access, Entry, and Hazards: Park along Highway 1; there is a short walk to the wide coarse sand beach. Watch for big surf, surge, and thick kelp. This is a dangerous beach entry due to the plunging breakers and unstable footing due to the coarse sand. Divers should be experienced with surf entries before attempting to dive here and should watch the surf before entering the water. Enter on either the north or south ends of the beach.

Cold-water divers should pay particular attention to their buoyancy when diving below 60 feet. As the depth increases, wet suit material becomes quite thin and loses buoyancy, requiring a substantial amount of air to be introduced into the BC. Divers should have a BC of sufficient capacity for this purpose and be skilled at maintaining proper buoyancy. In addition, as a wet suit compresses, it loses its insulating ability, so divers should plan on aborting the dive should they become hypothermic.

Monastery has a steep beach, producing plunging waves that break and disperse their energy over a very short distance. Conditions can change rapidly, so divers should be prepared for a rough surf exit even though their entrance was calm. The coarse sand found here causes unsure footing for divers as they stand in the surf line. The combination of coarse sand and rough surf has a tendency to inject sand into everything—up wet suits, down booties, throughout regulators, spearguns, cameras, etc. The locals have a endearing name for this sand — "Monster Berries."

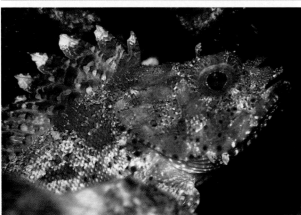

Mono-Lobo

One of my favorite spots is between Point Lobos State Reserve and Monastery Beach, and named appropriately Mono-Lobo. The Mono-Lobo wall is noted for its highly textured sides and its abundance of colorful marine life.

The wall begins as a ledge in about 40 feet of water that is dotted with huge granite outcroppings. These form a maze of canyons and are a real adventure to explore. Many of the rocks are carpeted with thick growths of strawberry anemones. These invertebrates are brightly colored in hues of red, orange, lavender, and pink, making spectacular subjects for underwater photographers. Other rocks are covered by orange volcano sponges, cobalt blue sponges, and an assortment of orange sea cucumbers. There is intense color wherever you look. It can be very dark during the summer and fall due to the thick growth of giant kelp. Divers may want to carry a flashlight to bring out the colors that are otherwise hidden by the kelp canopy.

As one approaches the edge of the kelp bed the bottom begins to drop away and fragment into many giant, granite pillars and massive rock formations before it plunges into the depths. Again, divers find an interesting bottom terrain of high-sided canyons, small caves and many deep recesses to explore. There is still a wealth of color at this depth as well. Along the exposed portions of the walls and in the surge channels are large trees of California hydrocoral. Hydrocorals only grow in areas of strong currents and areas that are free of pollution. They are a good indicator of the health of the reef.

Throughout the Mono-Lobo area the bottom drops in steps from 40 to over 120 feet, ending on a sand bottom. In most areas the wall resembles a broken talus field that one might expect to find in the mountains. Rock scallops hide in the deep recesses of the many nooks and crannies. In one spot the wall drops vertically from 40 to 100 feet and is encrusted with an assortment of anemones, sponges, and hydrocoral.

The whole Mono-Lobo area has an abundance of fish life. Large lingcod and cabezon hide among the rocks, while various species of rockfish occupy different places in the reef ecology. Blue rockfish hunt for jellyfish in the open water near the kelp beds; kelp rockfish feed on things that can be found on or among the kelp itself. Others, like gopher or black-and-yellow rockfish feed on the bottom.

Access, Entry, and Hazards. Mono-Lobo is a boat dive only, and the most comfortable way to dive here is from one of Monterey's charter dive boats. Watch for rouge waves and for thick kelp here.

Top: A rock covered with corynactis anemones and palm kelp.
Center: California scorpionfish. Bottom: Divers with purple hydrocoral.

Diving with Nudibranchs

I recall once giving a slide show on Philippine diving that featured a selection of colorful nudibranch photos. Afterwards, a diver asked me to suggest a spot closer to home where they might see nudibranchs like that. They were astonished when I suggested Monterey. So close and yet so unexplored to many!

Nudibranch means "exposed gills," and this order of mollusks consists of slug-like animals with outrageous coloring with both functional and decorative appendages. Members of all four suborders are found in Monterey, and each has its own charm and unique coloration.

Members of the dorid suborder are very common and can be seen grazing on algae-covered rocks or on sponges. This group of nudibranchs includes the bright-yellow, lemon nudibranch, and the white-and-black, ringed dorid. Dorids have two "horns" on the front end called rhinophores and a single ring of gills surrounding the anus. They are generally flat animals from the size of your fingernail up to the size of a large fist. Dorids are the most common suborder in Monterey, both by numbers of individuals and by numbers of species.

The generally more colorful and ostentatious group, the aeolids, are also quite common here. This suborder is characterized by four rows of gills running the entire length of the animal. The horned aeolid is particularly noticeable with its orange gills and yellow-and-blue-lined face. The Spanish shawl sports an outrageous purple body and orange gills and can also be observed in Monterey along with the red-and-white *Phidiana*.

Dendronotids are characterized by having spike-like gills that are not arranged in neat rows like the aeolids. Commonly seen species are the white *dendronotid*, Dall's *dendronotid*, and the rainbow nudibranch. Rainbow nudibranchs (*Dendronotus iris*) are found in the sandy areas. These large, 7-14 inch nudibranchs are a bright shade of red and owe their entire existence to burrowing anemones. The nudibranch will begin to feed on the anemone's tentacles and be drawn into the oral cavity of the anemone. It will then finish its dinner of fresh tentacles and crawl out of the anemone's tube. This usually does not kill the anemone, and in a few weeks it will grow its tentacles back. Not only do they eat the burrowing anemones, they also mate and lay eggs on them. The eggs of these nudibranchs are most often found draped around a burrowing anemone stalk and look like a mass of overcooked spaghetti.

Members of this suborder of nudibranch are capable of placing the stinging cells from the anemones that they consume onto the outside of their gill apparatus. This is a remarkable way of utilizing the defense mechanism of another creature. The stinging cells consist of a miniature poison-tipped, spring-loaded harpoon. It is not understood how the stinging cells are ingested by the nudibranch, while not being discharged, are yet deposited in the gills ready to fire.

The final suborder found in Monterey is *Arminacea*. This is the smallest of the suborders, both by individuals and species. There are only seven identified species in Monterey. *Arminacea* are best identified by having a physical appearance that does not fit into the other three suborders. The white-lined dirona is rare and may be found on deep, current-swept reefs. These are covered in white, plate-like appendages. Other *Arminacea (Armina)* can only be observed on sand bottoms at night.

Spanish shawl nudibranch.

Point Lobos State Reserve

Despite attempts by the California Department of Parks and Recreation to make the park look like nothing ever happened there, Point Lobos has enjoyed a colorful and busy history. In 1769 Point Lobos was first named "Punta de los Lobos Marinos," or Point of the Sea Wolves, by early Spanish settlers because of the large concentration of California sea lions that reside there. It was once the site of a stone quarry, which provided the foundations for many of the forts in the San Francisco Bay Area, as well as a logging camp, a whaling port, a coal mine, and an abalone cannery. Many of its owners did not appreciate the extent of the area's beauty and resources. Once, the land even changed hands in a deck of cards!

Fortunately, the State of California identified Point Lobos as a special place that needed protection as early as 1933 when it joined the state park system. In 1960, Point Lobos became the first underwater reserve in the nation when 750 submerged acres were added to the park. This occurred a full two years before the famed reefs at Pennecamp Coral Reef State Park in Florida achieved such status. In 1973 the Park was declared an ecological reserve, a move that protected all of the area's plants and animals from removal or disturbance. While it takes a keen eye to spot evidence of past human activity on land, divers continue to find metal artifacts throughout the underwater area.

Remember, authorities limit the number of divers that can visit the park on any given day. Reservations are required (see the "Summary of Monterey's Diving Regulations" section in the introduction chapter of this book).

Whalers Cove

Today Point Lobos State Reserve is known as a diver's area and Whalers Cove is the gateway to an underwater spectacle. The bottom of Whalers Cove consists of a sand bottom with dispersed rocky outcroppings. Thick beds of giant and bull kelp spring from these rocks and sea otters spend a lot of time napping among the kelp fronds. The kelp is quite thick in the summer and fall, sometimes making the cove inhospitable to surface-swimming divers.

From December through April leopard sharks enter the cove to pup. As many as 20, 3-to-5-foot, leopard sharks at a time may be seen in season in the shallow backwaters of Whalers Cove. Leopard sharks are live-bearers and seek out calm waters to deliver a dozen 4-to 6-inch young.

Harbor seals do not believe that leopard sharks make good neighbors and take a great deal of time to drive them from the cove. The seals will dive bomb the sharks as they rest on the sand bottom and blow bubbles at them. If all of that noise and commotion does not convince the sharks to leave, the seals will come up from behind the sharks, bite their tails, and chase them all of the way out of the cove. Because of this seal behavior, diver/photographers generally do better by free diving with these sharks rather than using scuba.

There are two small caverns beneath Coal Chute Point. The larger of the two is roughly shaped like a pyramid, with entrances at one point and the opposite base. The smaller entrance to the cave is located about 25 yards from the tip of Coal Chute Point on the Whalers Cove side of the Point, and is at or just below the water line depending on the height of the tide. This entrance is about seven feet wide and between two-to-three feet tall.

From the smaller entrance the cavern drops down 10 feet, turns right, and opens up into the pyramid-shaped main chamber, with slanted walls and a flat floor. The chamber continues to get larger as it proceeds through the point toward its second entrance in the small cove known as The Pit. This triangular-shaped entrance is about 40 feet on a side, and the bottom is in about 30 feet of water.

A diver explores a well-lit cavern.

Leopard shark.

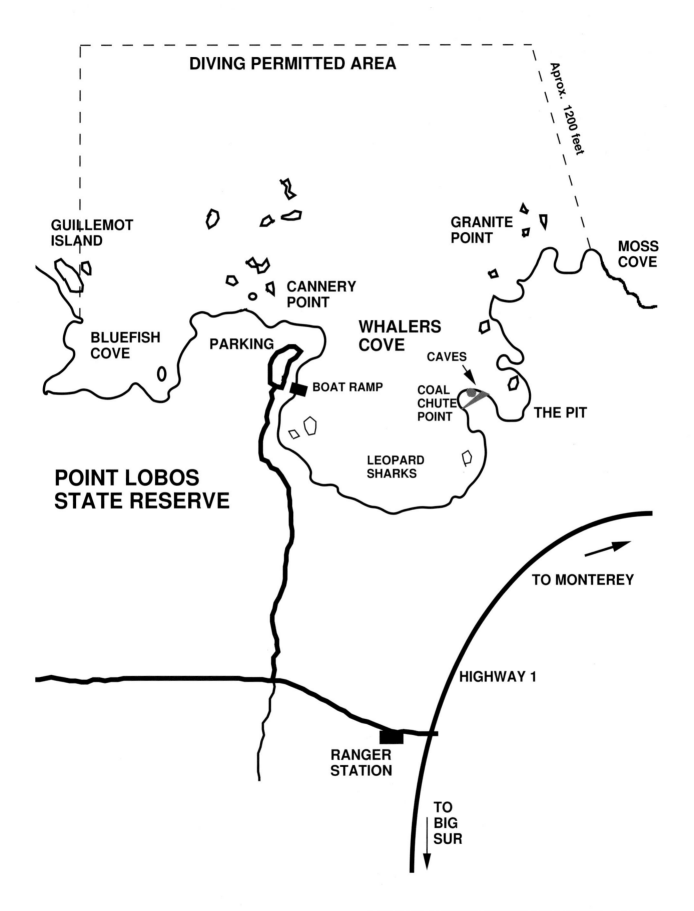

DIVING PERMITTED AREA

Aprox. 1200 feet

GUILLEMOT
ISLAND

GRANITE
POINT

MOSS
COVE

BLUEFISH
COVE

CANNERY
POINT

WHALERS
COVE

PARKING

CAVES

BOAT RAMP

COAL
CHUTE
POINT

THE PIT

POINT LOBOS
STATE RESERVE

LEOPARD
SHARKS

TO MONTEREY

HIGHWAY 1

RANGER
STATION

TO
BIG
SUR

Hydrocoral.

Purple sea urchin.

This cavern has no side tunnels and proceeds roughly straight through the Point with only one mild bend and runs about 80 feet, entrance to entrance. The walls of the cavern have some encrusting sponges in hues of yellow and red. On rough days divers should enter from The Pit side.

The second cavern is fish-bowl shaped and is about 30 feet across. It is located on the Pit side of Coal Chute Point, north of the larger cavern. This cavern has only one entrance and no blind passageways.

As cave diving goes, the caverns at Point Lobos are particularly safe to dive. Divers, nonetheless, cannot directly ascend to the surface in the event of an emergency, so proper precautions must still be taken. Buddy teams should be proficient in rescue skills, particularly in dealing with an out-of-air emergency situation, before entering this or any other cave or cavern.

The most colorful diving in Whalers Cove is on the west wall near the mouth of the cove. There are a series of rock faces in 30-50 feet of water that are covered with an assortment of colorful invertebrate life. Large rose-and white-spotted rose anemones dot the rock walls along with an assortment of delicate and colorful nudibranchs. Colorful sea cucumbers and encrusting sponges add color to your collection of macro photographs.

Since this is a reserve, the fish are not accustomed to being hunted and show little fear of divers; consequently, this is an excellent spot for fish photography. Large lingcod and cabezon peacefully rest on the bottom while thick schools of blue rockfish cruise just below the kelp canopy.

Access, Entry, and Hazards: Divers may only enter the water from the Whalers Cove boat ramp. This is a normally very calm cove; watch for thick kelp and boat traffic.

Bluefish Cove

As you continue to follow the rock wall at the mouth of Whalers Cove, the bottom gradually drops away to over 100 feet and wraps around to the left. That path leads one to the less touched and most outrageous diving of Bluefish Cove.

Along the west side of Bird Rocks stretches a rock wall that begins at 40 feet and drops vertically to over 100 feet. The entire surface of the rock is adorned with a multitude of striking colors. Thick carpets of red Corynactis anemones cover some areas, while red volcano or cobalt sponges cover others. Small crabs and an assortment of nudibranchs feed among the colorful collage. This is an excellent spot for macro photography. From the south side of the wall extends rocky ridges and channels that are home to an assortment of colorful anemones and the pink and purple hydrocoral.

Bluefish cove has direct assess to one of the branch canyons of the Carmel Trench, and as a result, an assortment of pelagic marine life can be found in the cove. While observing the interesting invertebrate life on the rocks, don't forget to turn around and look out into the open water. You may be able to catch a glimpse of a bat ray, sea lion, or basking shark as they pass by. Large Medusa jellyfish and schools of blue rockfish and anchovies are common.

This is an outstanding spot for fish photography. Since the fish here have never seen a speargun, they are not as afraid of divers as they are at nearby sites. Huge lingcod will sit still enough to allow you to photograph the copepods on their chins. Other fish will go about their day as if you're not there, allowing you to get good "behavior" shots. This is a great spot to observe cabezon guarding their nests.

Those with a boat will find the pinnacles and walls of Bluefish Cove are among the most beautiful in all of California. Large trees of pink and purple hydrocoral cover many of the rocky walls along with an assortment of colorful anemones. At least 50 of the 130 or so species of nudibranchs that inhabit California waters may be found here. Bluefish Cove is simply an awesome dive that overwhelms the senses in terms of color, variety, and excitement.

Access, Entry, and Hazards: Divers may only enter the water from the Whalers Cove boat ramp. On a calm day it is possible to swim to Bluefish by navigating between the Bird Rocks; however, this route should be avoided on rough days. Alternatively, divers can swim around the northern tip of Bird Rocks before submerging and heading south, or take their kayak or inflatable into the cove. Stay away from the wash rocks on rough days.

White-spotted rose anemone.

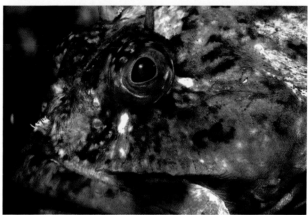
Cabezon face.

Above: Plume worm.
Left: Copper rockfish.

Introduction to Big Sur

When most divers think about Monterey the relatively small area of Monterey and Carmel Bays comes to mind. While these bays have many exciting dive sites, they represent only a small percentage of the beautiful Monterey county coastline. Most divers seem unwilling to cross the magic line at Point Lobos to explore sites farther south. And they certainly are missing a lot by not doing so. This "other Monterey" offers some of the best and untouched dive sites in all of California.

Each summer flocks of tourists descend onto the Big Sur coastline and navigate the curvy Highway 1 south of Monterey. For the most part they stop at the numerous turnouts, gaze upon what could be the world's most inspiring coastline, take a few pictures, and drive on. Waterfalls that drop onto white sand beaches and naturally sculptured cliffs textured with tunnels, caves, and arches beckon the visitors. However, the rugged landscape forces them to relish the splendor from afar.

The sheer cliffs of Big Sur still jealously guard these remote reefs. There are a few beach dives along the Big Sur Coast, but most of these are advanced double-diamond dives. This part of the Monterey Coast is most easily and most comfortably experienced from one of California's charter dive boats. These may be boarded either at Monterey or Morro Bay.

Big Sur diving is nothing short of spectacular. Offshore pinnacles dot the coastline and are covered with tapestries of colorful anemones and sponges; they are also accented with nudibranchs, decorator crabs, shrimp, and other photogenic creatures. The vertical cliffs hit the water and keep going down. Huge stands of California hydrocoral are common, a testament to the health of these waters. With little to no diving pressure over the years the area has truly exceptional game hunting. This remote coast produces huge lingcod and larger-than-average cabezon and rockfish, scallops, and abalone. With lack of river runoff the water here is exceptionally clear, and Mother Nature has thrown in a few shipwrecks for fun.

In the southern portion of the county, at the town of Lucia, the cliffs of Big Sur melt away into a area of rolling hills, short bluffs, and good beaches. Here the coastline of Monterey County is more like that of Southern than Northern California, and one finds a number of good diving areas with convenient shore access.

The rugged Big Sur Coast.

Gibson Beach

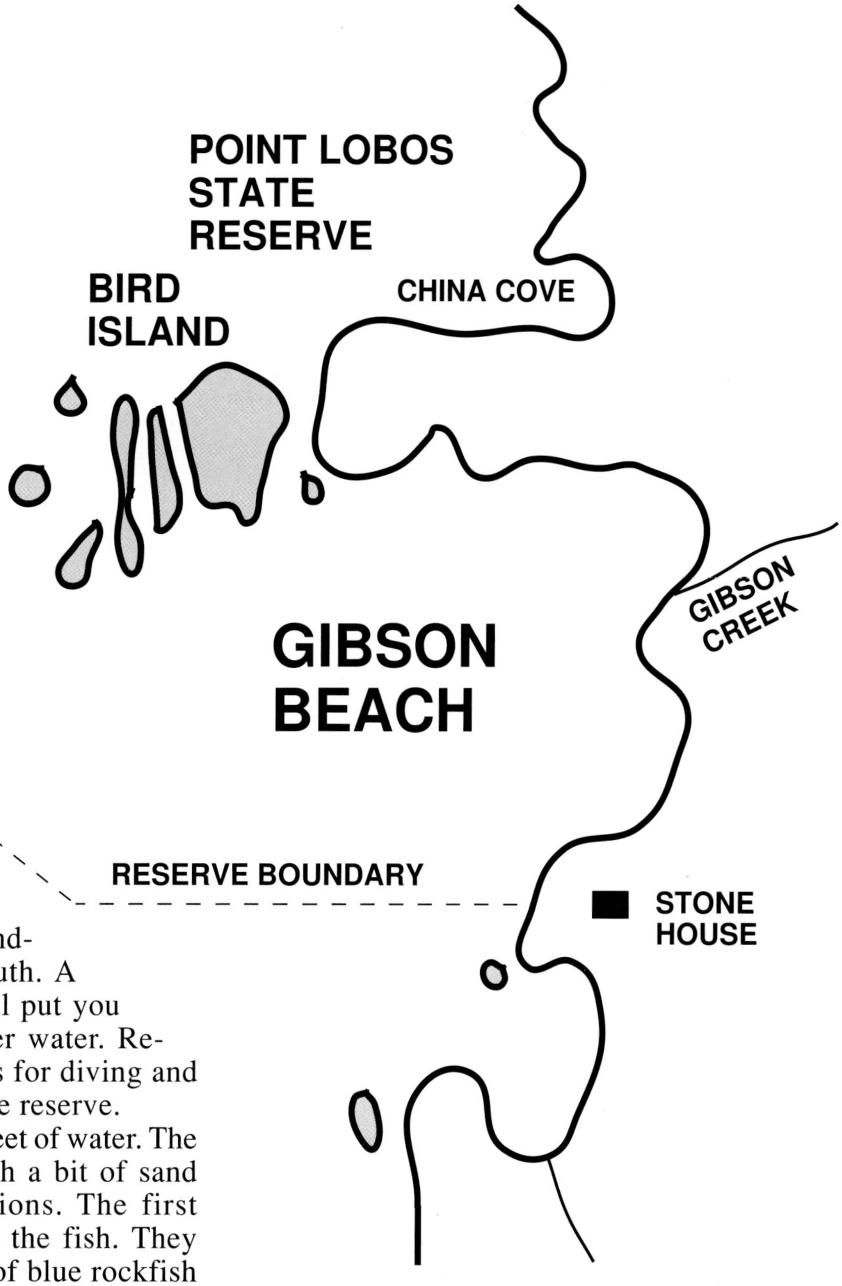

Gibson Beach is located just south of and adjacent to Point Lobos State Reserve. Divers should take heed as this site is located right next to the forbidden area of the reserve. Even divers entering through the reserve with permits cannot dive here. On the north side of Gibson Beach is a massive set of rocks that jut out into the Pacific. The largest is named "Bird Island" on the Point Lobos Reserve map and effectively protects the area south of the island from the northwesterly swell. This is a calm spot even on moderately rough days.

The Reserve boundary is the line drawn due west from the stone house directly south to the mouth of Gibson Creek. Charter dive boats normally anchor the boundary, and direct their divers south. A southwest compass heading will put you in good diving terrain in deeper water. Remember that there are stiff fines for diving and especially for spearfishing in the reserve.

Boats normally anchor in 40 feet of water. The bottom here is mostly rock with a bit of sand between massive rock formations. The first things you will notice here are the fish. They are everywhere. Thick schools of blue rockfish move among the kelp in shallow water. Big, fat, vermilion rockfish look like welcoming beacons perched on the tops of boulders. These brilliantly colored fish are as easy to spot as they are good to eat. They are very numerous here.

As you swim from the boat and head west you encounter one of the many rock fingers that originate at the beach and run parallel out into 90 to 100 feet of water. The sides of these fingers are vertical walls and are adorned with an assortment of colorful invertebrate life. Orange and yellow sponges cover some areas, while huge *Tealia* anemones form a monopoly in other locations. In deeper water large *Metridium* anemones dot the rocky walls and sift the water for plankton.

The scale of the reef is so overwhelming that you'll need to take some effort to notice the reef's small inhabitants. Little frilly nudibranchs, small reef fish, and an assortment of tiny crabs and shrimp are found on the walls. This is a good spot to photograph nudibranchs: you will find many colorful species such as the clown nudibranch dressed in orange and white; and the horned nudibranch dressed in yellow, orange and white with blue racing stripes.

Access, Entry, and Hazards: Boat Dive only. Watch for thick kelp and surge.

POINT LOBOS STATE RESERVE

BIRD ISLAND

CHINA COVE

GIBSON CREEK

GIBSON BEACH

RESERVE BOUNDARY

STONE HOUSE

Yankee Point

About one half mile offshore from Yankee Point is a massive, flat-topped underwater mountain. The top of this mountain is in about 60 feet of water and is, at first inspection, a flat plateau. A closer look reveals a massive granite structure deeply scored with deep canyons and valleys. Larger canyons rise 30 feet or so to the rim, and side valleys branch back into the rocky structure. The topography is similar to the Bad Lands of South Dakota and is an excellent place for wide-angle photography and exploration.

In shallow water the rocks support a layer of palm kelp. Below the layer of kelp the more shallow structures are covered with encrusting invertebrates. Colorful sponges, strawberry anemones, and coralline algae cover most every rock surface and seem to leave little room for sea stars, large rose anemones, and other critters. Yet, a closer look reveals tiny crabs, shrimp, nudibranch, and small fish tucked among the

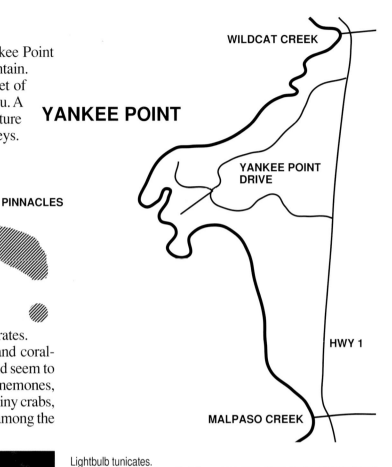

YANKEE POINT

WILDCAT CREEK

YANKEE POINT DRIVE

HWY 1

MALPASO CREEK

PINNACLES

A cabezon guards its eggs.

Lightbulb tunicates.

encrusting invertebrates. Game fish such as lingcod, cabezon, and vermilion rockfish hide among the palm kelp and rocky crevices. This is one of the most beautiful areas I've seen in California and is a great place for macro and fish photography.

On the inshore side of the area, the bottom drops off steeply to a sand bottom in about 100 feet of water. The nooks and crannies of the wall are home to an assortment of invertebrates and fish. A variety of nudibranchs are commonly found feeding on sponges, mating, or laying eggs. Orange sea cucumbers and rock scallops are found nestled in cracks. Rare to North/Central California, chestnut cowries are plentiful here in the recesses of the cracks.

On the outshore side of the rocky structure, the bottom drops off vertically to a little ledge at 120 feet, where it drops away again, and plunges to over 180 feet. The walls here are truly vertical, and diving here gives one the feeling of flying. Just off the wall you can soar with schools of blue rockfish, sometimes so thick they blot out the sun. Divers should look for pelagic animals such as the enormous lion's mane jellyfish and ocean sunfish.

By California Department of Fish and Game laws Yankee Point is the official divider between Northern and Southern California. It is therefore tempting for Monterey divers to compare this area to Southern California and the Channel Islands. But, make no mistake, this is neither Northern nor Southern California, but Central California, possessing the marine life from both areas.

Access, Entry, and Hazards: This is a boat dive only. Watch for currents and rough water. Nearby, boat-only sites are located offshore from Wildcat Creek and Malpaso Creek.

Garrapata State Park

The north boundary of Garrapata State Park is located just south of Yankee Point and about three and one half miles south of Point Lobos. It is somewhat of an anomaly among Monterey dive sites in that it offers some exceptional diving close to shore and has yet to be "discovered" by the diving community. When the parking lots at the Breakwater and Monastery beach have been filled since 7 o'clock in the morning and the reservation system has Point Lobos booked up two months in advance, you might find three or four divers at Garrapata. And, I say *might* because often you will see no other divers at all!

Garrapata is a big park, stretching for about four miles along Highway 1, and offers both a great number and variety of dive sites. Sites with names like "Mile Marker 67," "Moby Ling Cove," and

Chestnut cowry.

Kelp rockfish.

White-lined nudibranch.

Gray moon sponge.

"Reverse Cove" indicate the rough-and-ready personalities of the divers that first explored these waters.

Access, Entry, and Hazards: In general all of these sites share a number of features in common. They are at least 100 yards from the road and involve a little scrambling to get from the bluff face to the water. Sturdy shoes are recommended. The paths from the road to the water are lined with poison oak. You should make sure that no skin below the waist is showing. Lastly, this part of the coast is exposed to the prevailing surf. It can get rough here, and conditions can change rapidly. It is recommended that divers be experienced in rock entries and that first-timers bring along someone who is experienced with the area. Divers should be aware of currents, big swell, and surge.

Mile Marker 67

Divers should park near the "Mile Marker 67" sign. This is near the second dirt turnout after the northern boundary of Garrapata State Park. The trail to the entry point winds to the right of a large pine tree. This is easy to find since it is the only pine tree in the area. There is a steep climb to the water.

The entry point is at the end of a narrow chute. The chute can be surgy, but the conditions improve as you swim past the mouth and get into deeper water. The bottom consists of rock and sand and boulders. Depths range from 30 to 60 feet. This is a good area to spearfish for lingcod and rockfish. Non-hunters will be entertained by fish watching and admiring the abundance of encrusting and crawling invertebrates.

Waterfall Beach

The turnout to Waterfall Beach is about five miles south of Point Lobos along Highway 1, next to Mile Marker 66. Walk along a trail that runs along the south side of Soberanes Creek. From the trail you can see the creek as it dives to the beach in two cascades. At the bottom of the upper falls is a deep pool that is a perfect place to rinse off the salt after a day of diving. This pool is a little nicer in the spring as it tends to fill up with algae during

the summer.

This is a boulder-strewn beach, but entries and exits are fairly simple if the surf is not running. If the surf is up, you'll want to try another site. Off the beach lies a sandy bottom dotted with large pinnacles that gradually drops to about 60 feet. The pinnacles are a macro photographer's heaven. They are covered with a yellow encrusting sponge and an incredible wealth of crawly things. The colors are truly astounding. Many species of nudibranch, hermit crabs, and purple ringtop snails are found here in abundance. The fishing here is a little sparse, but the color of the rocky walls more than makes up for the lack of game.

WATERFALL BEACH

LOBOS ROCKS

PARKING

MM 66

ENTRY

ENTRY

MOBY LING COVE

SOBERANES POINT

ENTRY

OUTHOUSE

ENTRY

TRAIL

TREES

HWY. 1

REVERSE COVE

ENTRY

PARKING

Moby Ling Cove

Down the road a bit from Waterfall Beach is Moby Ling Cove. This site takes its name from a diver who was swimming back to the beach with a stringer of fish when a small gray whale passed directly underneath him! Park along side of the road where cypress trees are on both side of the road and just before you reach Soberanes Point. The trail begins right off the road and immediately splits. The path to the left takes you to Soberanes Point via an outhouse and the one to the right heads to Moby Ling Cove. The trail branches several times. Take the branches to the left, until you can see the cove, and then take the right branch.

A little scramble down a steep trail and some steps brings you to the easiest entry point I've ever seen, for two reasons. First, this cove is one of the most protected in the park. Second, it is a rocky point entry where divers only need to gear up and take a giant stride into eight-to ten-feet-deep water.

The shallow water near the entry point gives way to deeper water right when you get past the nearby wash rocks. Most of the cove is at about 50 feet. Directly underneath the first, flat wash rocks on the north side of the cove is a large underwater arch, some 40 feet long. The arch is so big that in low visibility it it possible to swim through it without noticing.

Once beyond the arch the bottom is mostly sand with a series of awesome pinnacles as the bottom drops from 20 feet to over 70. Most of the cove lies at about 50 feet. Macro photographers will find heaven on the rocks. Yellow encrusting sponges, red strawberry anemones, and red-and-white rose anemones are found here in abundance. There is so much color that you could easily spend an entire dive photographing the marine life on one small rock.

Soberanes Point

Soberanes Point is 4.7 miles south of Point Lobos along Highway 1. The parking area is marked by the large grove of cypress trees on both sides of highway. The long walk from the road to the entry point, about a third of a mile, is a level but strenuous walk in full scuba gear. The path to the right goes to the Moby Ling entry, and the one to the left goes to Soberanes Point. Divers should watch for large waves and surge. There is sometimes a swift current here. First-time divers to this site should find a buddy who has been there before. Alternatively, several of Monterey's charter boats dive this site.

Lingcod.

Spearfisher.

The bottom between the point and the offshore rocks consists of rock and sand that gently slopes from 50 to about 80 feet. Sprinkled on the flat bottom are numerous pinnacles that jut straight up to 30-40 feet from the surface. These pinnacles are covered with life. Chestnut cowries, uncountable species of anemones, sponges, crabs, nudibranchs: this place has everything. The marine life is so prolific here that every square inch of rock is covered. The competition for space is fierce. Some creatures have developed unique and deadly defense mechanisms. For example, *Metridium* anemones have specialized tentacles for warding off predators and claiming their "space" on the reef. The abundance of marine life and generally good visibility makes this a wonderful spot for both macro and wide-angle photography.

Because this site does not receive as many divers as nearby spots there is an abundance of game. Look for rock scallops under overhangs and cracks. If you look carefully you might see a few red abalone way back in the deepest cracks. Spearfishers should find productive hunting grounds here. Larger-than-average lingcod, cabezon, and rockfish are routinely taken here.

Diving with Sea Lions

Sea lions often announce their presence with barking that can be heard for some distance, both above and below the water.

Divers can get a close-up look of the herd as the sea lions sun themselves and an even closer look underwater. While normally shy when on land, the sea lions are at home in the water and lose much of their fear of humans. The sea lions will spend long hours playing games of hide-and-seek with divers and blowing bubbles in their faces. There is no need to chase after these mammals (illegal, anyway) as they will certainly come to you. One of my techniques for getting sea lion photographs is to pretend to be interested in something in a hole or on a rock. More often than not a sea lion will come right up to me and peer over my shoulder in order to see what I'm looking at.

Sea lions breed at offshore islands during the late spring and summer, so you should not expect to see many in Monterey from May through August. Afterwards, they return to the bay and fill up available haul-out spots on the breakwater and wharves. Sea lions generally feed at night and spend most of the day resting and sleeping. Sometimes they form large groups floating on the surface with one flipper in the air. The flipper acts as a solar collector to warm the sea lion.

Lobos Rocks

Lobos Rocks is a pair of rocks located offshore that jut up some 15 feet above the water line. Most of the diving here is on the large kelp bed on the south side of the rocks. Here divers find steep-sided deep canyons and walls that plunge to over 100 feet and are covered with an incredible carpet of invertebrate life. Pink and purple hydrocoral may be found here in abundance, a testament to the pollution-free conditions. Large *Metridium* anemones dot the canyon walls with their fluffy white tentacles catching whatever planktonic species drift by. Rose and spotted rose anemones are found in the surge channels and actively feed on fish and other larger prey as well. Huge lingcod lurk among the cracks and crevices. The spearfishing here is also quite good for cabezon and an assortment of rockfish and perch.

A colony of seal lions call these rocks home and often choose to follow divers along the bottom. If you are spearfishing they will frequently steal your catch.

Rose anemone.

Reverse Cove

Divers should park on the turnout on the west side of Highway 1 on the south side of Soberanes Point. Walk north along the guard rail and follow the trail to the small cove. The trail is very steep and slippery, and divers should be very careful. At the end of the trail is a small cove with a pretty, sandy beach. The cove is very well protected from a westerly or northwesterly swell, but is open to a southerly swell. This is normally a very easy entry once you haul your gear to the beach.

The bottom consists of rock and sand, and you have to swim a bit to get into deep water. The shallow water in conjunction with the steep trail makes this a better place for snorkeling than tank diving. Divers will enjoy spearfishing for rockfish and exploring the interesting bottom topography.

Diablo Pinnacles

The Diablo Pinnacles are a pair of rocks located south of Soberanes Point and offshore from the Granite Canyon Bridge. In summer the pinnacles can easily be located by the thick, offshore kelp bed. Diablo Pinnacles reach up from a 100-foot bottom to about 20 below surface and can only be reached by boat. This area is a relatively flat rocky plateau that drops off to 90 feet on the inshore side and to over 140 feet on the ocean side. The rocky bottom on the top of the pinnacles is marked with small canyons filled with large rose anemones and some pink and purple hydrocoral. The area supports a hefty concentration of large lingcod and cabezon. Because of the proximity to open water, pelagic species such as ocean sunfish and the enormous lion's mane jellyfish are often seen here.

Access, Entry, and Hazards: Boat dive only. Watch for boat traffic and strong currents.

Julia Pfeiffer Burns State Park.

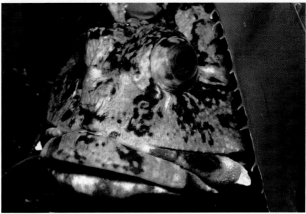
Cabezon.

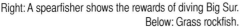
Right: A spearfisher shows the rewards of diving Big Sur.
Below: Grass rockfish.

Ventura Rocks

It is a time-honored tradition with cartographers to name offshore rocks in honor of ships that sunk there. Charts covering the Point Sur area show a pair of rocks about two miles north of the point and about a quarter mile offshore. These rocks take their name from the *SS Ventura* who ran aground here on April 20, 1875.

Ventura Rocks are a group of three pinnacles. Two of these break the water and the other's top is 30 or so feet below the surface. The largest rock juts about 20 feet above the water and is home to a small colony of California sea lions. The middle rock is just south of the big one and is above the water but is almost always awash.

Inshore around the rocks is an 80-foot, flat rock bottom with few good-sized boulders strewn about. The bottom is dotted with a few anemones and has the usual assortment of small fish and nudibranchs typical to Central California.

The ocean side of the rock has an absolutely flat and vertical surface. The wall begins above the water line and drops straight down to 140 feet. And I do mean *straight*. The rock looks like someone polished the entire surface smooth and straightened it with a plumb line. I've never seen a natural formation that was so big, so smooth, and so vertical. It's like diving on a polished Half Dome.

The surface of the vertical surface is covered with a carpet of red Corynactis. In fact this is the only invertebrate covering here. Just one sheet of anemones covering the entire rock face. It is a bit surprising that there is so little fish and invertebrate life here. Perhaps the polished surface offers few places to hide, or perhaps the charter fishing boats hit this area pretty hard. Even without an abundance of life, this is a wonderful place to experience. A flat red wall on one side and the open ocean on the other.

Just north and a bit west of the two main rocks is another pinnacle that begins on the 80-foot bottom and juts up to about 30 feet from the surface. The marine life here is much more interesting than the main rocks, although the topography is not so dramatic. This smaller rock is more craggy and textured and is home to rock scallops, nudibranchs, numerous encrusting invertebrates, and small fish.

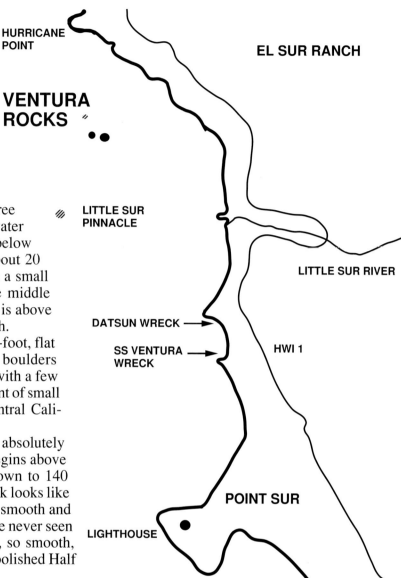

There is a noted absence of large game fish. On a recent coastal exploration trip, the photographers/sightseers voted this the best spot in the Big Sur Coast.

Just to the south and a bit offshore of Ventura Rocks and in line with the Little Sur River Canyon is the Little Sur Pinnacle. In the summer it may be located by the only wisp of kelp in the area. The south side of the pinnacle contains a large cave lined with *Metridium* anemones. The invertebrate life here is outstanding!

Access, Entry, and Hazards: This can be a very rough place to dive since there is no protection from the wind or swell regardless of directions. There is no shore access so this is a boat dive only. However, on a good day with clear water Ventura Rocks provides a marvelous site to explore and take in some very spectacular underwater scenery.

Wreck of the *SS Ventura*

During the late 1800s steam ships became commonplace along the California Coast. These mainly used coal for power, but also carried sails for those occasions when the engines failed to start or to save expensive coal during downhill runs. One of these was *SS Ventura* , a 230-foot-long wooden-hulled steamer built for the Navy during the Civil War.

The Navy sold her in 1873 to the Goodall, Nelson & Perkins Steamship Company for $41,000. Deck guns were removed, the double horizontal engine was replaced with the new triple expansion type, and accommodations for 78 cabin passengers and 200 passengers in steerage were added.

On Tuesday morning, April 20, 1975, the *Ventura* left San Francisco for Los Angeles with a planned stop in Santa Barbara. She carried 145 passengers and 400 tons of rugs and break-down wagons. The *Ventura* ran into a fog bank just past New Year's Island, but Captain Fake did not find it necessary to be on the bridge and chose instead to get liquored up with the ladies.

At about 8 p.m. the fog lifted, and the *Ventura* struck a rock, bounced off, and the mate put the ship in hard reverse. She backed into another rock, and the next series of waves swung her around and cradled her between two rocks. At that point the *Ventura* was stuck hard on the rocks. The crew panicked, boarded the two best lifeboats and left. The passengers and captain spent the night on the ship and were rescued the following morning.

Afterwards, the seas came up and drove the *Ventura* onto the beach stern first and bow into the waves. The vessel sank in only 15 feet of water and broke up under the onslaught of waves. As the cargo began to wash ashore the locals picked up what they could. Break-down wagons from the Ventura were reputedly in use along the coast for many years after the sinking.

Today, much of the wreck sits in 6 to 20 feet of water. The larger pieces of machinery are in plain view in a raised rocky area in about 15 feet of water, and, except for a layer of marine growth, are easily recognizable. A large brass cylinder, some six feet long and three feet in diameter, is cradled in a clump of rocks. This was probably part of the steam condenser. A large mass of iron (probably the steam engine) can be seen as well. These are often visible from the surface but are sometimes covered with sand.

A large metal pipe (probably the drive shaft) can clearly be seen from the surface protruding

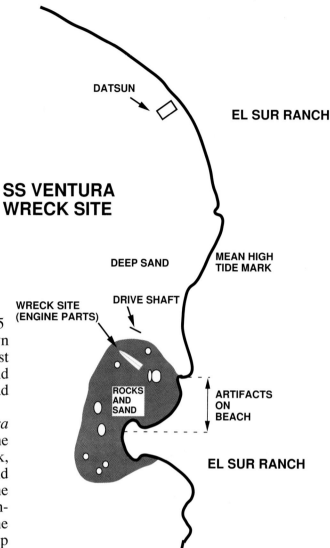

from the sand bed just north of the main site. Numerous small artifacts (brass fittings and portholes) and deposits of concretion could be found in the shallows. This area is in the surf zone, and the artifacts are constantly being moved around by wave action.

Artifacts are found on the beach at low tide. Iron pipe and fittings have formed concretion and have cemented many of the shore rocks together. None of the iron objects are recognizable. One piece of brass pipe about eight inches in diameter and two feet long can be found among the beach rocks. One end of the pipe has intact flange and the other is roughly broken. Samples of rust and concretion can be found on the beach from the south side of the little cove, south for about one-quarter mile.

Access, Entry, and Hazards: Access is by boat only. The *Ventura* can be a dangerous place to dive because the beach offers no protection from the swell and the wreck is so shallow.

Partington Cove

Also known as Smuggler's Cove, this site is in the northern part of Julia Pfeiffer Burns State Park, 36 miles south of Carmel. The diving here is quite good with a series of rocky ridges and pinnacles that jut up from the 30-60 foot bottom to within 20 feet of the surface. The rocks are painted with yellow and orange encrusting sponges and corals. Spearfishing for lingcod is excellent. A 70-foot-long cave passes through the point itself but is too dangerous to enter.

This state park may very well have the most stunning coastline in all of California, and has more than its fair share of arches and caves and waterfalls. Here McWay Creek flows to the cliff face, overshoots the cliff, and plunges over 100 feet to the beach below. This is the only spot in California where a waterfall drops directly into the ocean. The McWay Waterfall can be viewed from above from a lookout west of Highway 1, but the more spectacular view is from the beach. The only safe way to get to the base of this spectacular waterfall is from a boat. It is possible, but dangerous and forbidden by State Park rules, to climb down the loose and crumbly cliff to the beach.

Access, Entry, and Hazards: Diving here is by permit only (see the "Summary of Monterey's Diving Regulations" section in the introduction chapter of this book). Follow the fire road that begins on the south side of the bridge over Partington Creek, through the locked gate, and drops 200 feet to a parking area. Walk 200 feet through a 110-foot-long tunnel and enter the water from the rocky point. This is a very dangerous dive; I have witnessed several expert divers (e.g., instructors) get trashed in the waves here. Divers should avoid the area of the tunnel at all cost. The full force of the ocean swell is focused into a V-shaped cove into the tunnel, and two divers have died here.

Map

HWY. 1

DIRT ROAD

LOCKED GATE

ENTRY

PARTINGTON POINT

PARKING

TRAIL

NORTH COVE

TUNNEL

TRAIL

SAND

SEA TUNNEL

SOUTH COVE

ROCK AND KELP

ENTRY

SAND

ROCK AND KELP

45 FEET

PARTINGTON COVE

Cabezon.

Sea otters.

Slate Rock

One of the more typical spots along the Big Sur Coast is Slate Rock. This solitary rock sits about a quarter mile offshore and a little less than three miles south of Julia Pfeiffer Burns State Park. The rock stands offshore far enough to be constantly swept by currents. This currents brings nutrients to the critters living on the rock and creates a vibrant reef community.

The bottom around the rock gently slopes upward toward the shore line with ledges and large rocks and boulders. The depth around the base of the rock is about 60 feet and the bottom gradually drops off to 80 or 90 feet toward the seaward side.

This is a great place for spearfishing. Large lingcod are found here year round, and it is easy to shoot two or three, 28-inch or bigger fish on a single dive. There are large numbers of blue rockfish around the rock. The big attraction is not the blues

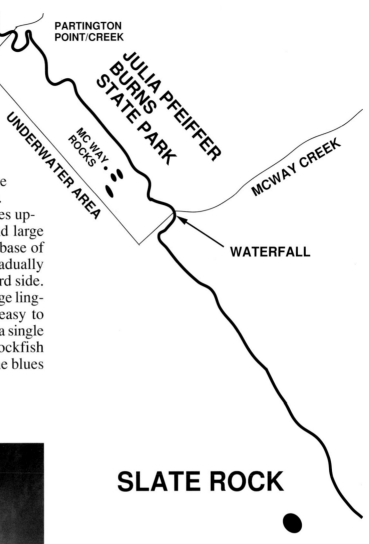

PARTINGTON POINT/CREEK

JULIA PFEIFFER BURNS STATE PARK

UNDERWATER AREA

MC WAY ROCKS

MCWAY CREEK

WATERFALL

SLATE ROCK

Below: Moon jelly.
Lower right: Kelp forest.

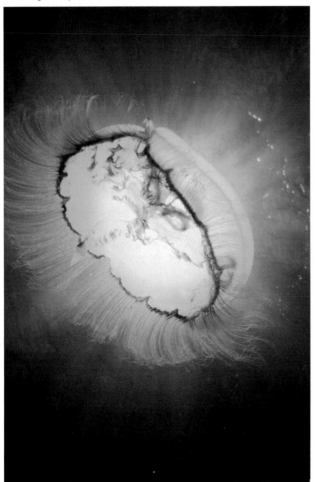

but the vermilion (reds) rockfish. These are also found here in large numbers and are considered to be one of the most worthy rockfish to hunt.

This rock supports one of the more diverse collections of little critters anywhere. In one small area I counted six species of nudibranchs: *Phidiana*, *Hermissenda*, clown, white-spotted, white- lined and lemon nudibranchs. And, there was not just one of each species, but rather at least two, and up to ten. This is nudibranch heaven.

Access, Entry, and Hazards: This site is accessible by boat only. Divers should watch for currents and thick kelp.

The beach at Mill Creek.

Limekiln Beach

This is another good spot to launch an inflatable boat, but beware of the unpredictable surf that can easily flip a boat. The area has an extensive kelp bed with rocky patches separated by sand and has excellent spearfishing for lingcod and rockfish.

Access, Entry, and Hazards: Access is through a private campground and beach may be reached by turning east from Highway 1, two miles south of Lucia and following the road that passes underneath the bridge. Small boats may be launched here. Watch for surge and big surf.

Mill Creek

A dive board or inflatable boat is needed to adequately explore this huge diving area. The bottom consists of rocky patches separated by stretches of sand in 25 to 60 feet of water. The pinnacles rise up 25 feet above the bottom and are covered with a colorful assortment of starfish, anemones, and sponges. The spearfishing here is excellent, and stringers of large lingcod, cabezon, and assorted species of rockfish are common. In the sandy patches between the rocks, halibut in the 30-to 50-pound range are found in summer.

Access, Entry, and Hazards: A pair of signs a mile apart mark a U.S. Forest Service picnic area and campground five miles south of Lucia. Follow the road down to a parking lot adjacent to the small beach and picnic area. Alternatively, divers may gain beach access by entering through the National Forest's Kirk Creek Campground, one mile north of the Mill Creek Picnic Area. Divers may park on the 100-foot bluff and take the steep trail to the beach. Watch for thick kelp and surge.

Sand Dollar Beach

Sand dollar beach is a beautiful sandy beach about one mile south of the town of Gorda. The near-shore beach has little to offer divers unless they are looking for sand dollars. There is a nice rocky area to dive along the south point of the cove where a healthy kelp bed and good invertebrate life, including some abalone, may be found. Spearfishing here may be good at times. This beach is one of the most protected in the area, but generally has reduced visibility.

Access, Entry, and Hazards: Park in the large lot 1.5 miles south of Gorda and hike the quarter-mile to the bluff and 100 feet down the well-maintained trail and stairs to the beach. Alternatively, you may follow the poorly maintained trail to the point and climb the bluff. Watch for surge and swell.

Sand Dollar Beach.

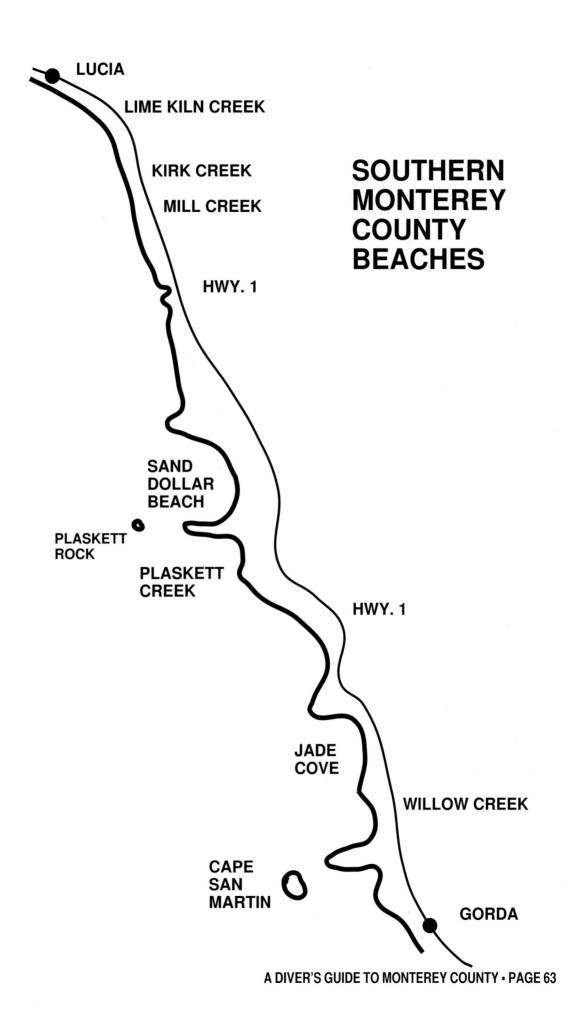

LUCIA

LIME KILN CREEK

KIRK CREEK

MILL CREEK

HWY. 1

SOUTHERN
MONTEREY
COUNTY
BEACHES

SAND
DOLLAR
BEACH

PLASKETT
ROCK

PLASKETT
CREEK

HWY. 1

JADE
COVE

WILLOW CREEK

CAPE
SAN
MARTIN

GORDA

Jade Cove

Jade Cove is actually two small coves. The beach consists of large boulders and coarse gravel. Jade hunters need not be divers as tide poolers regularly find many small jade pebbles at low tide between the boulders and in the gravel areas. But the better stones are found by divers.

Fifty yards offshore and to the left of the gravel beach is a large rock named Cave Rock. At the inshore base of the rock in about 20 feet of water is a cave that runs straight through the rock, parallel to shore. The inside surface of the rock is lined with polished jade. To the south of Cave Rock is a large gravel area where small pieces of jade may be easily found.

The bottom of the cove consists of many large rocks and boulders with gravel areas scattered about. The rocks are covered with red coralline algae and palm kelp. The cove is thick with kelp, particularly during the summer months, and giant, bull, and feather boa kelp are all common here. This cove is not very well protected from the deep ocean swell; and when the swells get big the broken pieces of kelp collect in

A diver displays a stone of jade.

Diving For Jade

Small pebbles of jade may always be found in the gravel beds within the cove, particularly the one near the cave rock and the one near the north point of the cove. Gently fan the gravel while looking for that characteristic jade color, or dig out a gravel bed with a small shovel. The large pieces can be anywhere. Search under large rocks and overhangs. If it is a particularly calm day look in shallow water that is not diveable when the surf is running, and is therefore not accessible on most days. Diving in the calm weather after a large storm can be the most rewarding time to find jade since the rough water usually exposes many previously hidden pieces.

Much jade has been removed from Jade Cove over the years, and the largest piece taken to date was a 9,000-pound boulder. The story describing how the jade was landed by a group of divers is told by Don Wobber in his book *Jade beneath the Sea*. This is a fascinating tale of how the divers removed the jade from the ocean, and their subsequent legal battle with the State of California to keep it. The Jade now rests in an Oakland museum, but for a while it was listed in the *Guinness Book of World Records* as the world's largest gemstone, until it was beaten in 1978 by a 143-ton piece from China.

the shallow water. The thick soupy mess is called "Minestrone Kelp" by jade divers.

Among the nooks and crannies of the bottom live an assortment of fish and invertebrates. Large ling-cod and cabezon may be seen patiently waiting for a small fish or crab to venture by. Colorful snubnose sculpins and painted greenlings hide among the cor-alline algae, while schools of blue rockfish and señorita move through the kelp canopy. Numerous species of nudibranch, bright orange sea cucumbers, as well as giant green anemones, are also common but often go unnoticed as divers single-mindedly hunt for jade.

Access, Entry, and Hazards: Park near the Na-tional Forest sign that announces Jade Cove. A trail leads from Highway 1, across a meadow, and down a 100-foot bluff. This trail is not for the faint-of-heart or the out-of-shape, as it is quite strenuous to haul your gear up from the beach. Divers should wear sturdy shoes. The cove is not very well protected from the predominantly northwesterly wind and waves and can get very rough and surgy. Even on the best of days surge can be a problem in the cove. Divers should be proficient in rocky entries and exits. A thick bed of kelp covers the cove in summer, so divers may want to carry a compass and allow enough air to get to the beach while staying below the surface. The best time to dive Jade Cove is from late summer through late fall, and between winter storms. Because of the lack of protection that the cove offers be pre-pared to find alternate entertainment on days when the cove is blown-out.

Cape San Martin

Cape San Martin is the most southerly site cov-ered in this guide and is about ten miles north of the San Luis Obispo County Line. The dive site is marked by a Coast Guard Beacon and a large offshore wash rock.

The bottom around the wash rock is about 40 feet deep and is composed of rock piles and a jumble of large boulders. Within the labyrinth of rocks is a pro-ductive nursery and condominium for bottom fish. Enormous lingcod are everywhere, and there is an incredible abundance of rockfish. This site has more vermilion rockfish (reds) than any other site I've seen in California. They are everywhere. On a recent coastal exploration trip we dived at most of the sites between Morro Bay and Point Sur, and the spearfishers rated this the best site.

Within the nooks and crannies of the rock piles are also found most of the species of nudibranch, shrimp, crabs, sponges, and anemones that are indig-enous to Central California. Macro photographers are

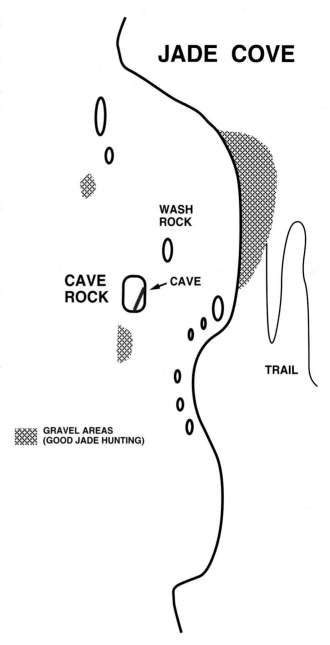

advised to bring enough film since the diversity and abundance of invertebrate life is hard to beat.

On the outshore side of the wash rock the rocky bottom gradually drops to a flat sand bottom in 80 feet of water. Spearfishing in these deeper waters is also quite good. Many find it comfortable to circum-navigate the wash rock during one dive.

Access, Entry, and Hazards: This is a boat dive only; there is no shore access. Boats can find good anchorage in the lee of the wash rock. This site is frequented by charter boats from Morro Bay, but it's a long way from the Monterey breakwater. Small, private boats may be launched from Mill Creek. Divers should watch for strong currents and surge.

Blue shark.

Offshore Diving: Diving With Sharks

If I had to pick the best dive in Monterey County, I would be hard pressed to come up with one site that stands above the rest. All of the sites described in this book are unique and have something different to offer the diver. Not every site is a good dive on any given day.

However, if I had to pick the most exciting place to dive in the county, the choice would be an easy one. I would head offshore. In reality, this is no site at all, and yet it covers the entire county. I prefer to be more than a mile out and sometimes four or five miles. This is in part because I don't want to constantly move the boat as it drifts toward shore, and partly because I like getting away from it all.

Blue water diving may be either feast or famine, depending on the day; however, if you see anything at all it is sure to be exciting. The offshore environment is mostly empty water dotted with interesting critters. You may run into members of the many species of jellyfish that inhabit the bay, maybe a by-the-wind-sailor, or maybe a pelagic tunicates or salp. But, the real reason to come here is for the big critters—sharks!

One of the least understood of California's off-shore animals is the **basking shark** *(Squalus maximus)*. In the early part of this century huge numbers of basking sharks cruised the waters of Monterey Bay. Reports from that time suggested that a single fisherman might spot as many as 1,000 animals a day. Basking sharks are the world's second largest fish (the whale shark is the largest) and can grow up to 45 feet long and weigh over four tons. They sift the water for plankton just below the surface, and often their large dorsal fin breaks the surface. Their gill rakers allow them to strain some 2,000 tons of water per hour.

During the late 1940s and 50s, a commercial fishery was established. The sharks were easily harpooned from the surface. The entire animal was then rendered down for oil, which was processed into aircraft lubricant. By the end of the 1950s only a few sharks remained in the bay, and spotter planes were used to pick off the few remaining animals. The sharks rarely came to the surface at that time and spotter planes allowed boat crews to harpoon deep-swimming animals. The harpooner did not even see the animal he was aiming for.

By the end of the '50s sightings of basking sharks in Monterey Bay stopped, and it was not until 1976 that a dozen animals were spotted off Carmel. By January of 1991, the numbers in the bay increased to 60, and over 100 animals were spotted during the

Basking shark.

The most common shark on these trips are **blue sharks** *(Prionace glauca)* although makos and whites are sometimes encountered. Blues are nothing short of poetry in motion. With a minimum of body movement they effortlessly glide through the water and their iridescent color sparkles in the sunlight. A blue's behavior toward divers is one of restrained curiosity rather than aggression, and most divers thoroughly enjoy the experience.

Shortfin mako sharks *(Isurus oxyrhincus)* are probably not more dangerous than a blue, but they look frightening. Their mouth is agape with jagged teeth pointing in every direction (surely an orthodontist's nightmare). They're also a fast and nervous shark. One minute they're in front of you, and the next, they're behind you. Diving with makos is exciting.

On rare occasions divers encounter the **great white shark** *(Charcharodon carcharius)* on these offshore trips. These are normally an inshore shark and are commonly found in shallow water near marine mammal haul-outs. Underwater a diver can only be amazed with the size and power of a white. They are thick, heavy-bodied animals that are incredibly impressive when viewed either from above or below the water. A diver is truly lucky to get a glimpse of these animals from the safety of a shark cage.

Divers often ask how to avoid being bitten by a shark. The only true shark repellent is the shade of an oak tree (oak trees don't grow near salt water); which is another way of saying don't go near the water if you're afraid of sharks. On the other hand divers are rarely bitten by sharks, and you're certainly at greater risk of dying in an automobile accident driving to the dive site than being bitten by a shark. Also, sharks rarely bite more than once, so dive with a buddy and they can pull you back to shore or your boat.

My best advice to avoid shark attack is not to dive at locations where shark attacks are common (there are no such locations in Monterey County). It is tempting to try to correlate shark bites with the activity of the victim, but in reality there is too little data available to draw hard conclusions. Attacks correlate with numbers of people in the water. As the number of people taking up diving, surfing, swimming, and other water sports increases, there will be more shark attacks, simply because there is a greater number of people in the water. Diving around large concentrations of natural prey (like seals and sea lions) is a risk factor.

winter of 1991.

Basking sharks appear seasonally, during the winter months in Monterey Bay and other places along the west coast of both North and South America. It is speculated that they spend the winter months off California and then migrate north to Washington and British Columbia during the spring and summer. It is believed that basking sharks lose their gill rakers when the levels of plankton drop. There is some speculation that the sharks either become dormant and hibernate on the bottom in deep water, or become bottom feeders while their gill rakers grow back.

Basking sharks are not protected at all under U.S. law. Some of the sharks we see are covered with monofilament fishing line and one had five arrows stuck in it. These are the results of hopeless attempts by fishermen to land these animals. Several others had mutilated dorsal fins as the result of close encounters with boat propellers.

We had the most delightful experience spending two full days with the basking sharks one December. I will always remember that Christmas Eve as the most exciting time that I ever spent in the water. We had 15 animals swim with us for the entire day. The smallest was about 20 feet long and the largest a bit over 30. All one had to do was to float in the water and the sharks would come right to you.

Some kinds of sharks can be observed and photographed simply by being in the right place at the right time. To get close to other types, however, particularly shy animals, you must draw them near you. You must bait them.

Typically dive boats head three to eight miles offshore and chum with a mixture of chopped fish. Dogma has it that you must be in water that is over 200 feet deep and warmer than 62° F (16.6° C) to find sharks.

Index

Page numbers in *Italics* indicate photograph